CAMBRIDGE PRIMARY
Global Perspectives

Learner's Skills Book 4

Adrian Ravenscroft & Thomas Holman

CAMBRIDGE
UNIVERSITY PRESS

Shaftesbury Road, Cambridge CB2 8EA, United Kingdom

One Liberty Plaza, 20th Floor, New York, NY 10006, USA

477 Williamstown Road, Port Melbourne, VIC 3207, Australia

314–321, 3rd Floor, Plot 3, Splendor Forum, Jasola District Centre, New Delhi – 110025, India

103 Penang Road, #05–06/07, Visioncrest Commercial, Singapore 238467

Cambridge University Press is part of the University of Cambridge.

It furthers the University's mission by disseminating knowledge in the pursuit of education, learning and research at the highest international levels of excellence.

www.cambridge.org
Information on this title: www.cambridge.org/9781108926713

First published 2021

20 19 18 17 16 15 14 13 12 11 10 9 8 7 6

Printed in Malaysia by Vivar Printing

A catalogue record for this publication is available from the British Library

ISBN 978-1-108-92671-3 Learner's Skills Book 4 Paperback with Digital Access (1 Year)

Contents

Introduction vii

How to use this book viii

Acknowledgements x

1 Research

Starting with research skills: Lesson 1 1
Starting with research skills: Lesson 2 6
Starting with research skills: Lesson 3 11
Developing research skills: Lesson 4 16
Developing research skills: Lesson 5 20
Developing research skills: Lesson 6 24
Getting better at research skills: Lesson 7 30
Getting better at research skills: Lesson 8 34
Getting better at research skills: Lesson 9 38

2 Analysis

Starting with analysis skills: Lesson 1 44
Starting with analysis skills: Lesson 2 49
Starting with analysis skills: Lesson 3 53
Developing analysis skills: Lesson 4 59
Developing analysis skills: Lesson 5 64
Developing analysis skills: Lesson 6 68
Getting better at analysis skills: Lesson 7 74
Getting better at analysis skills: Lesson 8 79
Getting better at analysis skills: Lesson 9 84

3 Evaluation

Starting with evaluation skills: Lesson 1 89
Starting with evaluation skills: Lesson 2 93
Developing evaluation skills: Lesson 3 99
Developing evaluation skills: Lesson 4 103
Getting better at evaluation skills: Lesson 5 108

4 Reflection

Starting with reflection skills: Lesson 1 113
Starting with reflection skills: Lesson 2 117
Starting with reflection skills: Lesson 3 121
Developing reflection skills: Lesson 4 126
Developing reflection skills: Lesson 5 130
Developing reflection skills: Lesson 6 135
Getting better at reflection skills: Lesson 7 141
Getting better at reflection skills: Lesson 8 145
Getting better at reflection skills: Lesson 9 149

5 Collaboration

Starting with collaboration skills: Lesson 1 154
Starting with collaboration skills: Lesson 2 158
Developing collaboration skills: Lesson 3 164
Developing collaboration skills: Lesson 4 169
Getting better at collaboration skills: Lesson 5 174

6 Communication

Starting with communication skills: Lesson 1 181
Starting with communication skills: Lesson 2 185
Developing communication skills: Lesson 3 191
Developing communication skills: Lesson 4 196
Getting better at communication skills: Lesson 5 202

Glossary 207

Introduction

Welcome to Stage 4 of Cambridge Primary Global Perspectives. If you are new to this course, you might be wondering 'What is it about?' A perspective is a view of the world – it is what you think and feel about the things that are going on in the world around you. As you progress through this book, we hope that you will explore your own personal perspectives on the topics. We also hope that you will begin to understand other people's perspectives, which may be different from yours.

To begin with, 'other people' might include your classmates, your family and friends, and people who live in your local area. However, we hope that you will also begin to explore the perspectives of people who live in other parts of the world. That is one reason why the word 'Global' is also in the title. Understanding each other's perspectives is important because people need to be able to work together to solve many of the world's problems.

To help you achieve this understanding, you will use and develop six important skills: Research, Analysis, Evaluation, Reflection, Collaboration and Communication. Each skill has its own section in this book, and each section is in three stages: 'Starting with', 'Developing' and 'Getting better at'. For each lesson, you will find clear learning goals. These will help you to reflect on your progress and decide how you can improve. In this way, you will also create a record of your learning as you work through the book.

The activities in each lesson will help you to develop the six Cambridge Global Perspectives skills. In each lesson, the focus is on one main skill, but you will use more than one skill most of the time. For example, many of the lesson activities ask you to work with others in your class in pairs or groups. That means you will be able to develop the skills of collaboration and communication while, at the same time, focusing on another skill, such as research or analysis.

In each of the lessons, you will find four characters (Zara, Arun, Marcus and Sofia). These characters will show you examples of the kind of work you will do in that lesson. They will also help you to start thinking about your own personal perspectives on the topics.

Remember that Cambridge Global Perspectives is also about finding out how other people think and feel in order to understand the world around you. Sometimes that means that you will need to work outside the classroom – at home, in your school or in your local neighbourhood. You might need to do this in order to get information or so that you can do things that will make a difference in the real world. Cambridge Global Perspectives is more than just learning about skills – it is also about learning how we can use those skills to make the world a better place.

We wish you every success in using this book to develop your Cambridge Global Perspectives skills. We hope that these skills will help you to grow and improve as a learner in the classroom, and also as a citizen of Planet Earth.

Adrian Ravenscroft and Tom Holman

How to use this book

This book contains lots of different features that will help your learning. These are explained below.

These are the learning objectives that will be covered in each lesson.

Research learning objectives

1.1 Constructing research questions

You can use these learning goals to identify what you are learning in the lesson, and how you know when you have met your goals.

Lesson learning goals

These are the goals for this lesson.
You will return to this table at the end of the lesson for the independent reflection activity.

My learning goals To get better at:	I think	My teacher/ partner thinks
discussing why other people do things, and how their actions affect others		
deciding the most effective action I could take to make a difference to a local issue		

These are questions or tasks to help check what you already know before beginning a lesson.

Prior learning

What do you think good teamwork looks like?

On a piece of A4 paper, draw one or more pictures to show your ideas.

Talk to a partner. Explain what your pictures show about good teamwork. Listen to what your partner tells you about their pictures. Do you agree?

New and important words are orange in the text. You can find out what they mean in the glossary at the back of the book.

Then reflect on the following:

In this lesson, you have considered how different countries make use of unequal resources. Then reflect on the following:

This helps you check how you are learning, and think about how well you are progressing with each goal at the end of each lesson.

Independent reflection activity

Check your learning goals

If you are sure you have met them and can give a reason why put a '★'.

If you think you have met them put a '☺'.

If you think you are not quite there yet put a '☹'.

This allows you to consider your progress through the learning goals in a deeper way. The table encourages you to think about where you are on your learning journey, and give examples to show how you are progressing. You can choose goals to improve on in the future.

Self-assessment Lessons 1–2

How will I know if I have achieved my learning goals?

Use this activity to reflect on how well you have progressed over the last two lessons.

Tick (✓) 'Achieved' if you are sure you have made good progress with this skill and can give an example.

Tick (✓) 'Not there yet / with help' if you need some further practice so that you can make more progress.

If you tick 'Achieved', then challenge yourself to make further progress in the next section.

If you tick 'Not there yet / with help', there will be the chance to consolidate this skill in future lessons.

Communication learning objectives To start to:	Not there yet / with help	Achieved	Example
communicate information			
listen and respond			

This provides an opportunity to reflect on your Challenge topic as you progress through each skill.

Challenge topic review

Think about the Challenge topic you have been exploring and complete the following statements.

I was surprised to discover/explore that ....

....

I did not know ....

....

I now think ....

....

Register to access free supporting resources through Cambridge GO – the home for all of your Cambridge digital content. Visit cambridge.org/go

Acknowledgements

The authors and publishers acknowledge the following sources of copyright material and are grateful for the permissions granted. While every effort has been made, it has not always been possible to identify the sources of all the material used, or to trace all copyright holders. If any omissions are brought to our notice, we will be happy to include the appropriate acknowledgements on reprinting.

Thanks to the following for permission to reproduce images:

Cover by Omar Aranda (Beehive Illustration)

Donald Iain Smith/GI; Pixelfusion3d/GI; Pictures Ltd/GI; Jose Girarte/GI; FatCamera/GI; Moodboard/GI; Robert Daly/GI; AlexRaths/GI; Gideon Mendel/GI; Alistair Berg/GI; FatCamera/GI; Donald Iain Smith/GI; Marko Geber/GI; Hadynyah/GI; Mikkelwilliam/GI; Tom Odulate/GI; Jose Luis Pelaez Inc/GI; Tom Odulate/GI; Terry Vine/GI; H.Armstrong oberts/ClassicStock/GI; Sergio Amiti/GI; English Heritage/Heritage Images/GI; Paul Souders/GI; Images By Tang Ming Tung/GI; Dougal Waters/GI; Maria Fedotova/GI; Leren Lu/GI; Bashir Osman's Photography/GI; Radomir jovanovic/GI; Teamjackson/GI; Bim/GI; Leland Bobbe/GI; Bsip/GI; Morsa Images/GI; Floortje/GI; Colors Hunter-Chasseur de Couleurs/GI; Kali9/GI; David Soanes Photography/GI; Matteo Colombo/GI; Sshepard/GI; Clubfoto/GI; Yobro10/GI; Recep-bg/GI; Zuraisham Salleh/GI; Sdi Productions/GI; Sdi Productions/GI; Johner Images/GI; Oli Scarff/GI; Maria Symchych-Navrotska/GI; Imtmphoto/GI; Scshutter/GI; Hadynyah/GI; Kaveh Kazemi/GI; Fstop123/GI; Hadynyah/GI; Klaus Vedfelt/GI; FatCamera/GI; In Pictures Ltd/GI; Jacob Maentz/GI; Skynesher/GI; Monkeybusinessimages/GI; Marcus Valance/GI; FatCamera/GI; Halfpoint/GI; Kali9/GI; Klaus Vedfelt/GI; Sdi Productions/GI; ThomasVogel/GI; Creative Touch Imaging Ltd/NurPhoto/GI; Rosa Rendtorff/GI; Jose Girarte/GI; Robert Kneschke/GI; Ian Grainger/GI; Jgalione/GI; Loop Images/GI; Fatcamera/GI; Keystone-france/gamma-keystone/GI; Fuse/GI; Sovfoto/Universal Images Group/GI; Sdi Productions/GI; Leon neal/GI; Fatcamera/GI; Solstock/GI; Tatiana dyuvbanova/GI; Peter cade/GI; Fatcamera/GI; Keren Su/GI; Str/GI; Avalon_studio/GI; Kuritafsheen/GI; Wavebreakmedia/GI; Péter hegedüs/GI; Delta images/GI; Christophe boisvieux/GI; Nik taylor/education images/GI; Aj_watt/GI; Nimit virdi/GI; Jose luis pelaez inc/GI.

Key: GI= Getty Images.

Starting with research skills: Lesson 1

Research learning objectives

1.1 Constructing research questions

1.3 Conducting research

Lesson learning goals

These are the goals for this lesson.
You will return to this table at the end of the lesson for the independent reflection activity.

My learning goals To start to:	I think	My teacher/ partner thinks
make my own questions to help me find out about a topic		
carry out an investigation using my own questions		

Prior learning

Zara is thinking about how children can keep fit and healthy.
She thinks of six ways:

a Eat a lot of fresh fruit and vegetables ☐

b Play sport at least once a week ☐

c Avoid drinking sugary drinks ☐

d Spend plenty of time outdoors ☐

e Limit time spent on electronic devices ☐

f Sleep as many hours as possible at night ☐

Which of these do you think is the most important?
Give each a number from 1 (most important) to 6 (least important).

Talk to a partner.

What is your 'Number 1' way for children to keep fit and healthy? Why?

Are there other ways for children to keep fit and healthy that you can think of?

Starter activity

The topic I am working on today is:

....

Zara notices that some children do not have a healthy lifestyle.
She discusses this with her group. Read what they say, then think about the discussion questions that follow.

Some children are getting overweight because they don't eat a healthy diet and spend too long sitting down every day.
I agree. They're always on their phones or their computers, and they spend most of their time indoors.
You sound like my parents! But some children don't have the time or opportunity to do sports or physical activity.
Let's find out how children spend their time out of school hours, and try to help them become more active.

Class discussion

1 How can Zara and her group investigate how children spend their free time?
2 What questions could they ask?

Main activity

Zara and her group decide to make a questionnaire.
They have started like this:

Out-of-school activity	Number of hours / minutes per week	
How many hours per week do you spend . . .	Child A	Child B
1 Doing your homework		
2		
3		
4		
5		
6 Other		

In your group, finish making the questionnaire by adding your own ideas in rows 2 to 5.

You are going to use your questionnaire to interview other children.

What questions can you ask? Write an example here:

....

....

Each person in your group should try to interview at least two other children (A, B). Write their responses in the columns on the right.

Class discussion

1 What has your investigation found out?
2 How could you share this information with others?
3 If you could carry out this investigation again, what would you do differently?

Independent reflection activity

Check your learning goals

If you are sure you have met them and can give a reason why put a '★'.
If you think you have met them put a '☺'.
If you think you are not quite there yet put a '😐'.

Starting with research skills: Lesson 2

Research learning objectives

1.4 Recording findings

Lesson learning goals

These are the goals for this lesson.
You will return to this table at the end of the lesson for the independent reflection activity.

My learning goals To start to:	I think	My teacher/ partner thinks
use a simple chart or diagram to record results of research		

Prior learning

Zara and her group are planning an investigation. They have thought of some steps they should take. What order should they do them in? Number each step from 1 (first step) to 6 (last step).

- Interview some people ☐
- Think of some questions we can ask ☐
- Tell others what we found out ☐
- Decide on a topic we can investigate ☐
- Make a questionnaire ☐
- Record our results ☐

Talk with a partner.

What topic would you like to investigate?

What questions would you ask?

Starter activity

The topic I am working on today is:

....

Zara and her group interviewed ten children using a questionnaire about what they did in their time outside of school. They used a pictogram to record their findings. Study the pictogram and think about the discussion questions that follow.

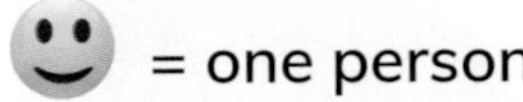 = one person

Out-of-school activity	Time spent each week		
	Less than 1 hour	1–3 hours	More than 3 hours
1 Doing your homework			☺☺☺☺☺☺☺☺☺☺
2 Doing sport or physical activity	☺☺☺☺☺	☺☺☺☺	☺
3 On your phone, computer or other device		☺☺	☺☺☺☺☺☺☺☺
4 Doing housework or chores	☺☺☺☺☺☺	☺☺☺☺	
5 Watching TV	☺	☺☺☺	☺☺☺☺☺☺
6 Other	☺☺☺☺☺	☺☺☺☺☺	

Class discussion

1 What can you learn from the pictogram?

2 What could be the reasons why some children do so little sport or physical activity?

3 What else could Zara and her group do to find out the reasons?

Main activity

Working with others in your group, make your own pictogram to show the results of the investigation you carried out in the last lesson:

Out-of-school activity	Time spent each week		
	Less than 1 hour	1–3 hours	More than 3 hours
1 Doing your homework			
2			
3			
4			
5			
6			

1 With the others in your group, decide on three things that you have learnt about what children do in their time outside school hours:

a ....

b ....

c ....

2 Write down a question about what children do in their time outside school hours that you would now like to investigate:

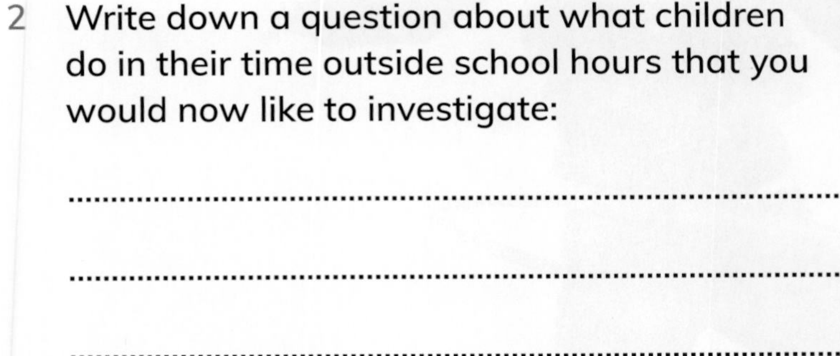

....

....

....

Peer feedback

Show your work from the Main activity of today's lesson to a partner from a different group, and ask them to tell you:

Two things that they like about your work (write what they tell you here):

★ ....

★ ....

One thing that you could improve (write what they tell you here):

 ....

Independent reflection activity

Check your learning goals

If you are sure you have met them and can give a reason why put a '★'.

If you think you have met them put a '☺'.

If you think you are not quite there yet put a '😐'.

3 Starting with research skills: Lesson 3

Research learning objectives

1.1 Constructing research questions

1.2 Information skills

Lesson learning goals

These are the goals for this lesson.
You will return to this table at the end of the lesson for the independent reflection activity.

My learning goals To start to:	I think	My teacher/ partner thinks
make my own questions to help me find out about a topic		
find information and answers to questions in a source		

Prior learning

Here are some sources about children's health and fitness that Zara and her group have found. Match the questions to the source that is most likely to give the answer. One example has been done for you.

Questions	Source number	Sources
a How can I get better at playing a team sport?	2	1 A children's website called 'Having fun outdoors'
b What is the best way to eat a balanced diet?		2 A TV programme called 'Basketball for beginners'
c Where can I find activities to do in the open air?		3 A book called 'Plan your day the healthy way'
d Who can show me what exercises to do to keep fit?		4 An online video called 'Work out with Jem B'
e When is the best time to do physical activity?		5 A magazine article called '10 healthy recipes for all the family'

Talk with a partner.

What other questions might you find the answers to in these sources?

Starter activity

The topic I am working on today is:

....

Zara and her group are looking for ways to help other children become more active and improve their health and fitness.

Here are some questions that Zara and her group would like to know the answers to:

a How much physical exercise should you do every day?
b What is the best way to improve your football skills?
c How can you limit the amount of time you spend looking at your phone?

d What type of physical activity helps you to keep fit and healthy?

e How can you use your phone or laptop to help you keep fit and healthy?

During their research, they find a website for children that includes a source with the title 'How children can keep fit and healthy in the digital age'. Look at Questions a–e above and think about the questions for discussion that follow.

Class discussion

1 Which of their questions do you think you might find the answers to in this source?

2 What other questions do you think it might have the answers to?

Main activity

Your teacher will give you the source 'How children can keep fit and healthy in the digital age' to read. Before you read it, write down three questions that you think this source might have the answers to:

a ....

b ....

c ....

Tick (✓) each question that you find the answer to.

Class discussion

1 Which of your questions did you find the answers to in the source?

2 What other questions did you find the answers to?

3 What questions would you still like to ask about children's health and fitness?

Independent reflection activity

Check your learning goals

If you are sure you have met them and can give a reason why put a '★'.

If you think you have met them put a '☺'.

If you think you are not quite there yet put a '😐'.

Self-assessment Lessons 1–3

How will I know if I have achieved my learning goals?

Use this activity to reflect on how well you have progressed over the last three lessons.

Tick (✓) 'Achieved' if you are sure you have made good progress with this skill and can give an example.

Tick (✓) 'Not there yet / with help' if you need some further practice so that you can make more progress.

If you tick 'Achieved', then challenge yourself to make further progress in the next section.

If you tick 'Not there yet / with help', there will be the chance to consolidate this skill in future lessons.

Research learning objectives To start to:	Not there yet / with help	Achieved	Example
construct research questions			
use information skills			
conduct research			
record findings			

Continued

Reflect on your responses in your self-assessment and identify one area for improvement.

One area I want to improve in is:

....

How I will improve:

....

Challenge topic review

Think about the Challenge topic you have been exploring and complete the following statements.

I was surprised to discover/explore that ....

....

I did not know ....

....

I now think ....

....

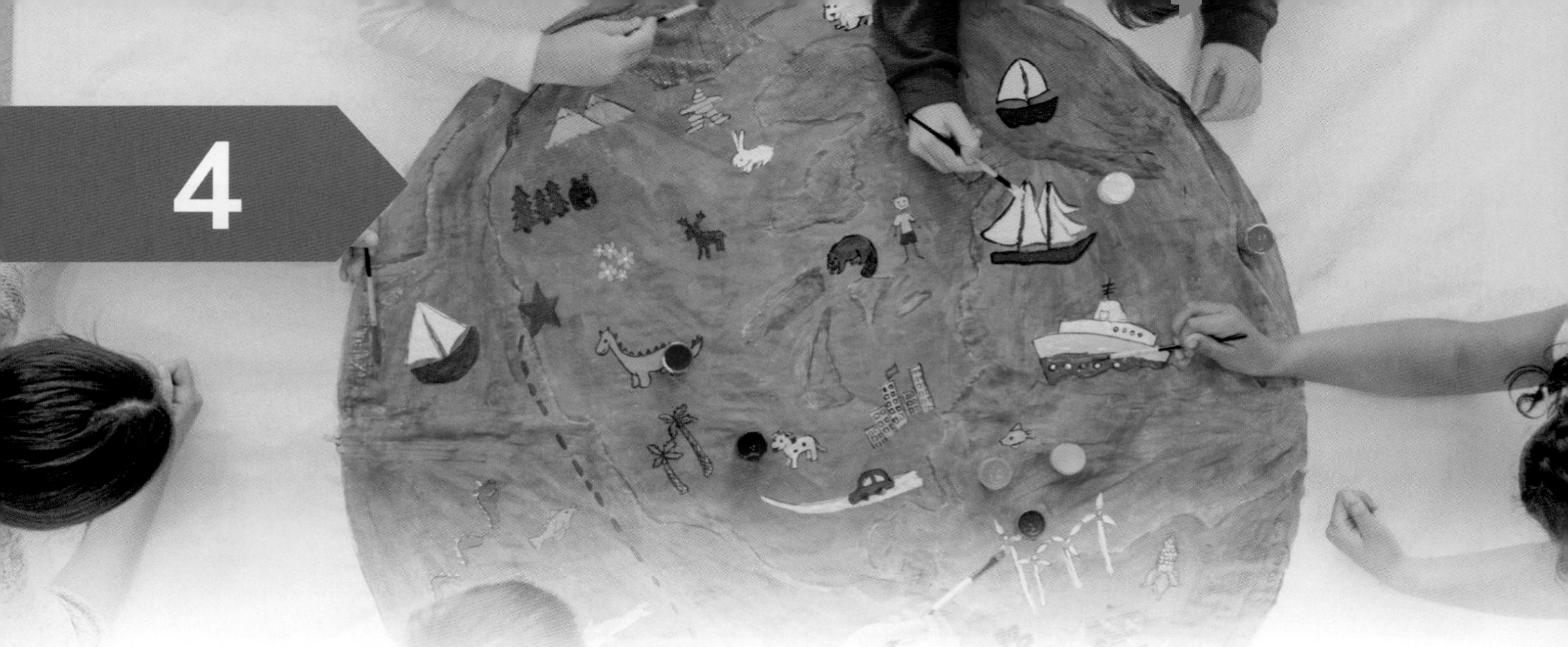

4

Developing research skills: Lesson 4

Research learning objectives

1.1 Constructing research questions

1.3 Conducting research

Lesson learning goals

These are the goals for this lesson.
You will return to this table at the end of the lesson for the independent reflection activity.

My learning goals To develop my knowledge and understanding about:	I think	My teacher/ partner thinks
how to make my own questions to find out more about a topic		
how to carry out an investigation using a questionnaire		

Prior learning

Zara and her group have been thinking about the topic of 'Keeping healthy'.

Zara: I think children around the world are pretty much the same. Some children don't look after themselves.

Sofia: I agree. It doesn't matter where they are – they're *exactly* the same.

Marcus: That's not quite right. Some children are active.

Arun: I totally disagree. There are massive differences around the world.

Based on your prior understanding, which member of the group do you agree with most? What are your reasons?

Note down your ideas ready for the class discussion.

Class discussion

Share your thoughts with the class. Be clear about whose viewpoint you agree with and why.

Starter activity

The topic I am working on today is:

....

Zara and her group gave reasons for their statements about children around the world. Who said what? Can you match the person to their reason?

Foods like pizzas, burgers and fried chicken are international. Often children are tempted to stick to them.

Wherever you go in the world, you see the same brands. Children follow the same lifestyle. You get the same results.

Games like football are popular all around the world and some children like them.

Climate makes a huge difference. There are some climates that make it nearly impossible to get outside. Some children just don't have access to things like games and phones, so they will be more active.

Main activity

If Zara and her group could get in touch with other children in different parts of the world, how could that help them find out which of their four statements is right?

What questions could they ask them? Make a list of questions you can think of on a sheet of A4 paper (the first three have been done for you):

a Do children like computer games or exercise where you live?

b Is unhealthy fast food becoming popular where you live?

c Does the climate where you live stop people from taking part in exercise?

Now choose three of your questions and adapt them so that they could be included in a questionnaire. Make sure your questions ask for an answer that is a number. For example:

a How many children in your class spend more time on computer games than exercise each week?

b How many children in your class eat fast food takeaways every week?

c For how many months a year is it possible to take exercise outdoors at your school?

Write your questions here:

a ....

b ....

c ....

Class discussion

1 What are the advantages of open questions?

2 What are the advantages of questions that ask for a number?

Independent reflection activity

Check your learning goals

If you are sure you have met them and can give a reason why put a '★'.

If you think you have met them put a '☺'.

If you think you are not quite there yet put a '😐'.

5

Developing research skills: Lesson 5

Research learning objectives

1.1 Constructing research questions

1.3 Conducting research

Lesson learning goals

These are the goals for this lesson.
You will return to this table at the end of the lesson for the independent reflection activity.

My learning goals To develop my knowledge and understanding about:	I think	My teacher/ partner thinks
how to make my own questions to find out more about a topic		
how to carry out an investigation using a questionnaire		

The topic I am working on today is:

....

Prior learning

Thinking about your topic, which statement best matches your opinion based on your prior knowledge and understanding?

a As far as this topic is concerned, it doesn't matter where you go; children are exactly the same.

b As far as this topic is concerned, depending on where you go, there are some differences, but children are mostly the same.

c As far as this topic is concerned, depending on where you go, there are some similarities, but children are mostly different.

d As far as this topic is concerned, it depends entirely on where you are; children are very different.

What are your reasons? Note down your ideas ready for the class discussion.

Class discussion

Share your thoughts with the class. Explain the reasons for your answer.

Starter activity

In the last lesson, Zara and her group gave reasons for their statements about children around the world. They focused on their topic of Keeping healthy. Can you summarise the reasons children in your group or class gave for their opinions about your topic?

Statements	Reasons
As far as this topic is concerned, it doesn't matter where you go; children are exactly the same.	
As far as this topic is concerned, depending on where you go, there are some differences, but children are mostly the same.	

Statements	Reasons
As far as this topic is concerned, depending on where you go, there are some similarities, but children are mostly different.	
As far as this topic is concerned it depends entirely on where you are; children are very different.	

Main activity

Getting in touch with other children around the world is a good way to find out more about your topic. It can help you to find out if the issues are similar or different in different places. If you could get in touch with children your age in different schools around the world and discuss your topic with them, how could you find out which of the four statements above is correct?
What questions could you ask them? Make a list on a sheet of A4 paper. Make sure you include some open questions and some questions that ask for a number. Now classify these questions into 'open questions' and 'questions that ask for a number' so that they you could use them in a questionnaire.

Class discussion

Share your questions with the class. Think about when open questions are useful and when questions that ask for a number are useful.

Peer feedback

Talk to a partner from a different group about what you did in this lesson.

Ask your partner to tell you:

Two ways that you developed your skills in conducting research (write what they tell you here):

 ....

 ....

One way that you could improve your research skills (write what they tell you here):

....

Independent reflection activity

Check your learning goals

If you are sure you have met them and can give a reason why put a '★'.

If you think you have met them put a '☺'.

If you think you are not quite there yet put a '😐'.

Developing research skills: Lesson 6

Research learning objectives

1.2 Information skills

1.4 Recording findings

Lesson learning goals

These are the goals for this lesson.
You will return to this table at the end of the lesson for the independent reflection activity.

My learning goals To develop my knowledge and understanding about:	I think	My teacher/ partner thinks
how to find information and answers to questions in one or more sources		
how to use simple charts or diagrams to record results of my own research		

Prior learning

Look back at the chart Zara's group compiled for their research on 'Out-of-school activity' in the Starter activity in Lesson 2.

Here are some statements about their findings. Assess these statements using the star-rating key provided below.

a The children surveyed spend more time doing homework than sport.

b The children surveyed spend more time doing sport than homework.

c The children surveyed enjoy TV.

d Homework is a higher priority than housework or chores.

Key

*** This statement is fully supported by the evidence.

** This statement is supported by the evidence.

* This statement could be supported by the evidence.

✗ This statement is not supported by the evidence.

Starter activity

The topic I am working on today is:

....

The team would like to find out more about how children around the world spend their time. They have written to their international partner schools and received some responses. Read Raoul's letter in the download that your teacher will give you.

How would you assess the way he describes the way children in his class spend their time compared to your own? Tick (✓) one.

	Totally different	Mainly different	Some similarities and differences (a balance)	Mainly similar	The same
1 Doing homework					
2 Doing sport or physical activity					
3 On a phone, computer or other device					
4 Doing housework or chores					
5 Watching TV					
6 Other					

Give reasons for your answer:

1 ....

....

2 ....

....

3 ....

....

Class discussion

What is your perspective? How does this compare to the class as a whole?

Main activity

Now read the responses from the other international partners.

Use the key and the table below to summarise your impressions of the four children's lives based on what they say in their letters.

Key

*** This seems to be a very important part of children's lives.

** This seems to be a quite an important part of children's lives.

* This does not seem to be such an important part of children's lives.

✗ This is not important.

? We have no information.

	Homework	Sport	Housework/ chores	Computer games	TV	Other pastimes
Raoul						
Priti						
Hong-Kai						
Afia						

Class discussion

The team have been discussing what they found out.

Who do you agree with most? Why?

The way the children spend their time is *completely* different.

I'm afraid I disagree, Zara; the way the children spend their time is completely *the same*.

Let's take a look. There are some things that are similar. There are mostly differences though.

I understand what you're saying. Some things are different. The way they spend their time is mostly the same though.

Independent reflection activity

Check your learning goals

If you are sure you have met them and can give a reason why put a '★'.

If you think you have met them put a '☺'.

If you think you are not quite there yet put a '😐'.

Self-assessment Lessons 4–6

How will I know if I have achieved my learning goals?

Use this activity to reflect on how well you have progressed over the last three lessons.

Tick (✓) 'Achieved' if you are sure you have made good progress with this skill and can give an example.

Tick (✓) 'Not there yet / with help' if you need some further practice so that you can make more progress.

If you tick 'Achieved', then challenge yourself to make further progress in the next section.

If you tick 'Not there yet / with help', there will be the chance to consolidate this skill in future lessons.

Research learning objectives To develop my knowledge and understanding about:	Not there yet / with help	Achieved	Example
constructing research questions			
using information skills			
conducting research			
recording findings			

Continued

Reflect on your responses in your self-assessment and identify one area for improvement.

One area I want to improve in is:

....

How I will improve:

....

Challenge topic review

Think about the Challenge topic you have been exploring and complete the following statements.

I was surprised to discover/explore that ....

....

I did not know ....

....

I now think ....

....

Getting better at research skills: Lesson 7

Research learning objectives

1.1 Constructing research questions

Lesson learning goals

These are the goals for this lesson.
You will return to this table at the end of the lesson for the independent reflection activity.

My learning goals To get better at:	I think	My teacher/ partner thinks
deciding what questions will help me find out most about a topic		

Prior learning

Sofia has been talking to her grandmother about what her life was like when she was a child and received the following answers. Which question (a, b or c) do you think Sofia asked to get each response? Tick (✓) the correct question.

1 'People used to eat more food that was cooked at home – not so much fast food and take-outs as nowadays.'

- a How have eating habits changed since you were a child? ☐
- b Do you eat the same things now as when you were a child? ☐
- c What are the things that you like to eat nowadays? ☐

2 'There used to be more local shops that you could walk to, so even if you had a car, you didn't need to use it all the time.'

- a Have you noticed any changes in the way people do their shopping? ☐
- b What did most people use their cars for when you were a child? ☐
- c Why do people use their cars more often nowadays? ☐

3 'We only had a TV in our living room, so everyone used to watch the same thing at the same time.'

- a How have people's homes changed since you were a child? ☐
- b What did your family do to entertain themselves at home? ☐
- c As a child, what was your favourite TV show? ☐

Talk with a partner. What other questions could you ask an elderly person about their childhood?

Starter activity

The topic I am working on today is:

....

Sofia is discussing the topic of children's physical fitness with her team.
Read what they say, and think about your answers to the questions that follow.

My grandmother says children were fitter in the past than they are now because they did more physical activity.

I can't believe that! Children in the past didn't have all the opportunities to do sport that we have nowadays.

Yes, but you have to remember that, these days, many children spend all their time indoors on their electronic devices.

This would make an interesting topic to investigate. I wonder how we could find out more about it.

Class discussion

1 Do you think that children are fitter nowadays than they were in the past? Why do you think this?
2 What changes have happened in children's lives since Sofia's grandmother was a child?
3 How could Sofia and her team investigate this topic?

Main activity

Sofia and her team plan to interview some elderly people, such as her grandmother, to find out more about how children kept fit in the past. They have made a mind-map with some topics they would like to find out about. Your teacher will give this to you.

Work in a group. What questions could Sofia and her team ask in order to find out more about the topics in the mind-map? Write your questions on the mind-map. Add other topics and questions that you would like to find out about.

Class discussion

Share your questions with the class.

1 What do you think the answers to your questions would be if you interviewed an elderly person?
2 How do children keep fit nowadays, and how is this different from the way children used to keep fit in the past?

Independent reflection activity

Check your learning goals

If you are sure you have met them and can give a reason why put a '★'.

If you think you have met them put a '☺'.

If you think you are not quite there yet put a '😐'.

Getting better at research skills: Lesson 8

Research learning objectives

1.2 Information skills

1.3 Conducting research

Lesson learning goals

These are the goals for this lesson.
You will return to this table at the end of the lesson for the independent reflection activity.

My learning goals To get better at:	I think	My teacher/ partner thinks
finding information and answers to questions in more than one source		
carrying out an investigation using an interview or a questionnaire		

Prior learning

For a school project, Marcus has been reading about national flags and making notes. He read this source about the flag of Nisu:

> The flag of the tiny island of Nisu is divided into three horizontal bands. The top band is blue, representing freedom and the tropical climate of the island. The bottom band is black, representing the rich soil of the island, where many crops are grown. Nowadays, it could also represent oil, which has been discovered in the seas around Nisu. The middle band is gold, representing the wealth and happiness of the islanders. In the centre of the flag, there is a circle containing an image of the red tautau flower on a white background. The tautau is the national flower of Nisu, and the fruit of the tautau tree is one of the island's main exports. Below the circle is a scroll containing the date '1959', the year when the island became an independent nation.

Marcus has started making notes from this source.
Complete his notes, using information from the source:

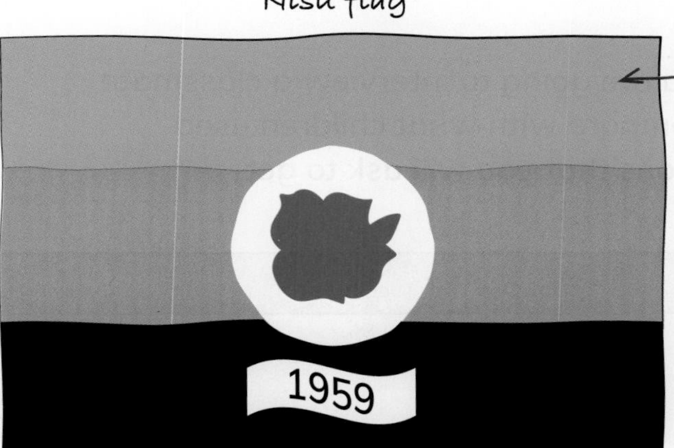

Talk with a partner. How would you describe your country's flag to Marcus?

Starter activity

The topic I am working on today is:

....

Sofia asked some of her friends in other countries to interview their grandparents about how they used to keep fit when they were children. Her friends wrote down what their grandparents told them.

Read the source that your teacher gives you from one of the interviews carried out by Sofia's friends. Make notes under these headings:

- Types of physical activity
- Keeping fit at school
- Keeping fit out of school
- Equipment used and kit worn

You may not find information for all of these headings in your source. Share what you've learnt with others in your group, and complete your notes by adding what they tell you.

Class discussion

What information have you found out about each of the headings?

Main activity

How do children keep fit nowadays? You are going to interview a classmate to get some information that you can compare with what children used to do in the past. Write down the questions that you will ask to get information about each of these topics:

Topic / Question	Response
Types of physical activity Q.	
Keeping fit at school Q.	
Keeping fit out of school Q.	

Topic / Question	Response
Equipment used and kit worn Q.	

Now interview a classmate and make notes of their responses in the space provided.

Peer feedback

Show your notes to a partner, and ask them to agree or disagree with these statements:

1 You've made questions that ask for useful information. YES/NO

2 You've noted down the information in the responses clearly. YES/NO

Ask your partner for one way that you could improve your questionnaire (write what they tell you here):

....

....

....

....

Class discussion

1 What important differences have you discovered in the way children keep fit now, compared to how they kept fit in the past?

2 What else would you like to investigate about this topic?

Independent reflection activity

Check your learning goals

If you are sure you have met them and can give a reason why put a '★'.

If you think you have met them put a '☺'.

If you think you are not quite there yet put a '😐'.

9

Getting better at research skills: Lesson 9

Research learning objectives

1.4 Recording findings

Lesson learning goals

These are the goals for this lesson.
You will return to this table at the end of the lesson for the independent reflection activity.

My learning goals To get better at:	I think	My teacher/ partner thinks
putting information in simple charts or diagrams to record results of my own research		

Prior learning

Look at the information you found out in the previous lesson about how children keep fit nowadays, and how they kept fit in the past.

Decide what you think the three most important differences are:

1 ....

2 ....

3 ....

Talk with a partner. Do you agree on what the most important differences are?

Starter activity

The topic I am working on today is:

....

Sofia and her team are discussing the topic of children's physical fitness. Read what they say:

Class discussion

1 What do you think the answer to Zara's question is?
2 What information could you use to persuade others to change their behaviour?

Main activity

Sofia and her team decide to make a poster showing the differences between how children used to keep fit in the past and how they can keep fit nowadays. Read how they want their poster to persuade children to do more physical activity:

This is what they plan their poster to look like:

Work in a group. Use the information you have researched in previous lessons about the past and the present to complete your own version of Sofia's group's poster.

Share your poster with others in the class.

Class discussion

Do you think this is a good way to persuade children to do more physical activity? Why?

Independent reflection activity

Check your learning goals

If you are sure you have met them and can give a reason why put a '★'.

If you think you have met them put a '☺'.

If you think you are not quite there yet put a '😐'.

Self-assessment Lessons 7–9

How will I know if I have achieved my learning goals?

Use this activity to reflect on how well you have progressed over the last three lessons.

Tick (✓) 'Achieved' if you are sure you have made good progress with this skill and can give an example.

Tick (✓) 'Not there yet / with help' if you need some further practice so that you can make more progress.

If you tick 'Achieved', then challenge yourself to make further progress in the next section.

If you tick 'Not there yet / with help', there will be the chance to consolidate this skill in future lessons.

Research learning objectives To get better at:	Not there yet / with help	Achieved	Example
constructing research questions			
using information skills			
conducting research			
recording findings			

Continued

Reflect on your responses in your self-assessment and identify one area for improvement.

One area I want to improve in is:

....

How I will improve:

....

Challenge topic review

Think about the Challenge topic you have been exploring and complete the following statements.

I was surprised to discover/explore that ....

....

I did not know ....

....

I now think ....

....

Starting with analysis skills: Lesson 1

Analysis learning objectives

2.1 Identifying perspectives

Lesson learning goals

These are the goals for this lesson.
You will return to this table at the end of the lesson for the independent reflection activity.

My learning goals To start to:	I think	My teacher/ partner thinks
describe what a person thinks or believes about a topic		

Prior learning

Marcus is thinking about what is fair and what is unfair.

1 When do you think you might have used the word 'fair' before?

Try to put it into a sentence you might have used: ....

....

2 When do you think you might have last used the word 'equal'?

Try to put it into a sentence you might have used: ....

....

3 Complete these sentences:

I know I am being treated fairly when ....

I know I am being treated equally when ....

Compare your answers with a partner. Be ready to share ideas in a class discussion – you will need to explain not just your own ideas but your partner's too.

Starter activity

The topic I am working on today is:

....

Read Marcus and Arun's diaries on the download that your teacher will give you. Then answer the questions on the next page.

1 What was the competition? ....

2 Who won? ....

3 Describe Arun's perspective on the competition.
Use the sentence starters to help you.

Arun feels that the competition was ....

This is because ....

He thinks that ....

The reason for this is that he believes ....

....

4 Describe Marcus's perspective on the competition.
Use the sentence starters to help you.

Marcus feels that the competition was ....

This is because ....

He thinks that ....

The reason for this is that he believes ....

....

Use these words to help you:

elated aggrieved fair unfair deserved
did not deserve equal unequal materials

Main activity

1 I think that the competition was:
An equal one ☐ / An unequal one ☐. Tick (✓) one.

2 Which perspective most closely matches your own about the hat competition described in the diaries:

Tick (✓) one:

1

It was completely fair. Everyone had the chance to make a hat. Arun's was clearly the best, so he deserved to win.

2

It was mainly fair. Although Arun had some good materials and others did not, his was still the best so he deserved to win.

3

It was mainly unfair. Arun's was the best, but he had materials that others did not – so he did not really deserve to win.

4

It was completely unfair. Everyone did not have the chance to be the best. Arun was bound to win because he had the best materials.

Discuss this with your group.

Now, after the discussion, do you still think the same way? You can change your mind, but you do not have to.

I now agree with perspective number .... the most.

The reason for this is that firstly, ...

In addition, ...

Furthermore, ...

Finally, ...

Share your ideas with two other people and be ready to report a range of perspectives to the class.

Class discussion

Be ready to share your perspective.

Use these sentence starters to help you.

The perspective I agreed with most was perspective number ....

I agreed with it because ....

....

However, ... [name of your first group member] thought that perspective number .... was most convincing.

They agreed with it because ....

....

Finally, ... [name of your second group member] thought that perspective number .... was the best thought through.

They agreed with it because ....

....

How could we encourage Marcus to adopt a more positive perspective?

We could encourage Marcus to ....

Independent reflection activity

Check your learning goals

If you are sure you have met them and can give a reason why put a '★'.

If you think you have met them put a '☺'.

If you think you are not quite there yet put a '😐'.

2 Starting with analysis skills: Lesson 2

Analysis learning objectives

2.2 Interpreting data

Lesson learning goals

These are the goals for this lesson.
You will return to this table at the end of the lesson for the independent reflection activity.

My learning goals To start to:	I think	My teacher/ partner thinks
describe what the data in a graph or chart shows		

Prior learning

Arun and his group have been thinking about data.

Arun: I used a tally chart when I was finding out about different kinds of shops on the high street. Clothes shops were the most common.

Zara: I used bar graphs to show which insects live in different places. I found they like the shade.

Marcus: I used a **Venn diagram** to help me sort 3D shapes. Spheres were hard to place.

Sofia: I used a line graph to show temperature. It got hotter in the middle of the day because the sun is high.

Make notes:

Think of a time when you used data.

What did you record? ....

How did you record it? ....

How did you present it? ....

What did you learn? ....

Starter activity

The topic I am working on today is:

....

You are going to complete a group challenge that your teacher will set you. Listen to what your teacher tells you and note down the following:

1 What equipment does your group have available?

....

2 How many learners are there in your group?

....

3 How will you help your group perform in the challenge?

....

Main activity

In your groups, complete the task that your teacher sets you.

When you have finished, consider how well your group and the other groups performed the task.

How did the other groups' performances compare with your group?

Group	Number in the group	Equipment	Points scored
A			
B			
C			
D			
E			
F			

Class discussion

The more equipment you have, the better your score will be.

Be ready to answer these questions:

1 Which group had the highest score?

....

2 Which group(s) had the most equipment?

....

3 Which group(s) had the least?

....

4 Did one of the groups that started with the most equipment have the highest score? YES/NO

5 Did one of the groups that started with the most equipment have the lowest score? YES/NO

6 Sofia tried this activity. She decided that 'The more equipment you have, the better your score will be.' Does your data back up her perspective?

Completely ☐ mostly ☐ partly ☐ not at all ☐ (Tick ✓ one).

Explain your answer: ....

Independent reflection activity

Check your learning goals

If you are sure you have met them and can give a reason why put a '★'.

If you think you have met them put a '☺'.

If you think you are not quite there yet put a '😐'.

3

Starting with analysis skills: Lesson 3

Analysis learning objectives

2.3 Making connections

2.4 Solving problems

Lesson learning goals

These are the goals for this lesson.
You will return to this table at the end of the lesson for the independent reflection activity.

My learning goals To start to:	I think	My teacher/ partner thinks
talk about my reasons for doing something that affects other people		
think of something I could do to make a difference to a local issue		

Prior learning

Think about your contribution to the group's task in the Main activity of Lesson 2.

1 What tasks did you perform?
2 How did they contribute to the group's achievement?
3 If you were to repeat the challenge, what aspects of the way you worked would you keep the same? Why is this?
4 If you were to repeat the challenge, what aspects of the way you worked would you change so that the group could do better? Why is this?

Starter activity

Arun has been asked about ways in which he makes a positive contribution.

He has filled in a table.

Where I made a contribution	In my home	In my community	To a different community
How I did this	I helped my younger brother and sister sort out the washing into different piles then I put them away. We made it into a game.	I made the drinks at the cricket tournament for the other teams.	We held a talent show for UNICEF last year. I sang a song with three of my friends.
Why I did this	They are too young to do this all by themselves, and they get bored easily.	Our club was the host for the tournament, and we wanted the other teams to feel welcome.	It was fun! But there was a serious point. We were raising money for children so that they can go to school.

Now think of an example of a contribution that you have made. It could be:

- in your home
- in your community
- to a different community.

Write it in the download that your teacher will give you. Explain how and why you performed the contribution.

Main activity

Zara, Marcus, Arun and Sofia have been thinking about issues in their community.

Not all children in our community have internet access. It means they find it hard to do their homework.

The local park is run down and people don't use it. They don't feel safe.

Some people don't have jobs.

There are people who are homeless.

Could we help? Why don't we find out more from a homeless charity?

Could we set up a computer club?

The topic I am working on today is:

....

What issues do people face in your community?
Have you got any ideas for action that could be taken?

Discuss your ideas with your group. Record the results of your discussion in the download that your teacher will give you.

Peer feedback

Show your work to a partner from a different group, and ask them to tell you the answers to these questions:

1 Have you identified at least one issue that people face in your community? YES/NO

Ask them to explain their answer and write down their reason here: ....

....

2 Have you identified at least one appropriate action that could be taken to improve your community? YES/NO

Ask them to explain their answer and write down their reason here: ....

....

3 Can they identify another appropriate action that could be taken? Or can they suggest a way of improving one that you thought of?

Ask them to explain their answer and write down their reason here: ....

....

Class discussion

What are the ideas that you have identified so far for practical action? (This could come from your own group or your peer feedback group.)

1 What do you think is the best idea?

2 Why is this?

3 What additional information could help you to make a more informed decision?

Independent reflection activity

Check your learning goals

If you are sure you have met them and can give a reason why put a '★'.

If you think you have met them put a '☺'.

If you think you are not quite there yet put a '😐'.

Self-assessment Lessons 1–3

How will I know if I have achieved my learning goals?

Use this activity to reflect on how well you have progressed over the last three lessons.

Tick (✓) 'Achieved' if you are sure you have made good progress with this skill and can give an example.

Tick (✓) 'Not there yet / with help' if you need some further practice so that you can make more progress.

If you tick 'Achieved', then challenge yourself to make further progress in the next section.

If you tick 'Not there yet / with help', there will be the chance to consolidate this skill in future lessons.

Analysis learning objectives To start to:	Not there yet / with help	Achieved	Example
identify perspectives			
interpret data			
make connections			
solve problems			

Continued

Reflect on your responses in your self-assessment and identify one area for improvement.

One area I want to improve in is:

....

How I will improve:

....

Challenge topic review

Think about the Challenge topic you have been exploring and complete the following statements.

I was surprised to discover/explore that ....

....

I did not know ....

....

I now think ....

....

4

Developing analysis skills: Lesson 4

Analysis learning objectives

2.1 Identifying perspectives

2.2 Interpreting data

Lesson learning goals

These are the goals for this lesson.
You will return to this table at the end of the lesson for the independent reflection activity.

My learning goals To develop my knowledge and understanding about:	I think	My teacher/ partner thinks
how different people think or believe different things about a topic		
how to identify useful data in a graph or charts to answer questions		

Prior learning

Think back to the Starter and Main activities in Lesson 1.
Prepare your ideas for a class discussion.

1 What was the issue? ....

2 Was there one perspective on this issue or were there several? ....

3 Why was this? ....

....

Starter activity

The topic I am working on today is:

....

Sofia, Marcus, Zara and Arun have been collecting data about the town they live in. They want to find out:

- whether older people can get to fresh fruit and vegetable shops easily
- whether poorer people can get to fresh fruit and vegetable shops easily.

They researched:

- where the different districts in their town are
- where older people live
- where poorer people live
- where the fresh fruit and vegetable shops are.

Look at their maps and tables (your teacher will give you these in a download). Now answer these questions:

1 How many vegetable shops are in District 5? ☐

2 What percentage of people in District 10 are over 65? ☐

3 What district has the most people over 65 living in it? ☐

4 What is the percentage of poor people living in District 4? ☐

5 How many districts have ten or more vegetable shops in them? ☐

6 How many districts have fewer than five vegetable shops in them? ☐

7 How many districts have more than 15 percent of people over 65 in them? ☐

8 Which two districts have the highest poverty rate? ☐

Main activity

Older people tend to live on the north side of town.

		YES	NO
1 a	Is Zara right?	☐	☐

b Explain how you know: ....

....

Younger people tend to be less poor in our town.

		YES	NO
2 a	Is Sofia right?	☐	☐

b Explain how you know: ....

....

			YES	NO	NOT SURE
3	a	Is Marcus right?	☐	☐	☐

b Explain how you know: ....

....

Poorer people have
fewer fresh fruit and vegetable
shops in their areas, and
that's not fair.

			YES	NO	NOT SURE
4	a	Is Arun right about the pattern in the data?	☐	☐	☐

b Explain how you know: ....

....

		YES	NO	NOT SURE
c	Do you agree with Arun's perspective?	☐	☐	☐

d Explain your perspective: ....

....

Class discussion

1 What did Zara, Sofia, Marcus and Arun want to find out?
2 What data did they collect?
3 How did Arun develop a perspective on the issue?
4 What do you want to find out?
5 What data would it be helpful for you to collect?
6 Have you developed a perspective on the issue?
7 Have you spotted any patterns in the data?
8 Do they support your perspective?

Independent reflection activity

Check your learning goals

If you are sure you have met them and can give a reason why put a '★'.

If you think you have met them put a '☺'.

If you think you are not quite there yet put a '😐'.

5

Developing analysis skills: Lesson 5

Analysis learning objectives

2.3 Making connections

2.4 Solving problems

Lesson learning goals

These are the goals for this lesson.
You will return to this table at the end of the lesson for the independent reflection activity.

My learning goals To develop my knowledge and understanding about:	I think	My teacher/ partner thinks
my reasons for doing things, and how my actions affect other people		
what different actions I could take to make a difference to a local issue		

Prior learning

Think back to the Main activity in Lesson 3. Make notes on the following:

1. What issues did you think affected your community?
2. What were the ideas that you had identified at that point for practical action? (This could have come from your own group or your peer feedback group.)
3. What did you think was the best idea then?
4. Why was this?
5. Do you still think the same way?
6. What additional information have you found out to help you to make a more informed decision since then?

Share your thoughts in a class discussion.

Starter activity

The topic I am working on today is:

....

Sofia has been thinking about her group's reasons for doing things, and how their actions affected other people. She wrote in her diary about actions she took to make a difference in her school.

1 Read the extract from Sofia's diary and answer the questions that follow.

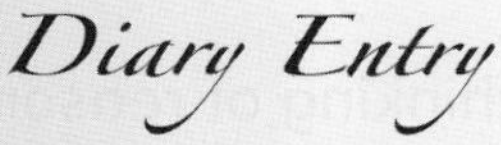

Wednesday 20th March

Today I went into Class 1b to be a reading buddy. I thought I would be good at this because I enjoy reading. This was the third time I'd done this. To be honest, I wasn't looking forward to it very much. The little girl I have been working with is called Shagufta, and she has been so shy. This time I let her choose, so we read 'Hairy McLary from Donaldson's Dairy' together. I couldn't believe it! She read some of the words all by herself – especially the bits where the story had a pattern. She giggled at some of the pictures 'Look! 'He's so so funny with the BIG bone!' I really think she is starting to like reading more now. I feel quite proud in fact.

Question	Answer
1 Where was the action taken?	Class 1b
2 Why did Sofia take the action?	
3 How was Shagufta affected by the action?	
4 How was Sofia affected by the action?	
5 What difference do you think Sofia's action made?	

2 Now think about your own reasons for doing things and how your actions have affected other people. Think about an action you have taken to make a difference in your school. Complete the table that your teacher will give you.

Main activity

Marcus has been thinking of reasons for taking action on a local issue and how his actions will affect other people. He has been thinking about actions he will take to make a difference in his community.

He has asked himself the following questions and noted his answers.

Question	Answer
1 Where will the action be taken?	In the old people's home
2 What will you do?	Sing some songs and stay to talk afterwards
3 Why will you take the action?	Because they can sometimes be lonely
4 What research have you done?	We have read a letter from the care home manager
5 How do you hope another person (or other people) be affected by the action?	They will get to meet some young people for a change
6 How do you think you will be affected by the action?	I might hear some interesting stories about the olden days
7 What difference do you think your action will make?	They may feel less lonely

Now think about your reasons for taking action on a local issue and how your actions will affect other people. Think about actions you will take to make a difference in your community. Answer the questions in the table that your teacher will give you.

Class discussion

Reflect on how you have developed your reasons for doing something and how your actions will have an impact on other people.

1 How do you know the action you plan on a local issue will make a real difference to people?

2 What further information can you find out to make sure?

Independent reflection activity

Check your learning goals

If you are sure you have met them and can give a reason why put a '★'.

If you think you have met them put a '☺'.

If you think you are not quite there yet put a '😐'.

Developing analysis skills: Lesson 6

Analysis learning objectives

2.1 Identifying perspectives

2.2 Interpreting data

Lesson learning goals

These are the goals for this lesson.
You will return to this table at the end of the lesson for the independent reflection activity.

My learning goals To develop my knowledge and understanding about:	I think	My teacher/ partner thinks
how different people think or believe different things about a topic		
how to identify useful data in a graph or chart in order to answer questions		

Prior learning

Look back at the data from the Main activity in Lesson 2.

On reflection, which group do you think worked the best?

....

What is the main reason for holding this opinion?

....

Find someone who disagrees with your evaluation.
Describe what they think or believe about this topic:

....

Or if you can't find someone who disagrees with your evaluation, describe what a different perspective on this topic *could* be:

....

Share your answers in a class discussion.

Starter activity

The topic I am working on today is:

....

Your teacher will give you a download containing data on various countries. The countries are made up, but they are based on real places. Look at the data and answer the following questions.

1 Which country has the highest Gross Domestic Product (GDP)? ....

2 Which country has the highest number of doctors per capita? ....

3 Which country has the lowest GDP? ....

4 Which country has the lowest number of doctors per capita? ....

5 How many countries on the list have GDP below $5000? ....

6 How many countries on the list have fewer than 1 doctor per 1000 people?

....

Main activity

		YES	NO
1	a Is Zara right?	☐	☐

b How do you know? ....

Use the sentence starters to help you develop your answer.

The pattern I can see in the data is that ....

For example, ...

We can also see that ....

An example of this is ....

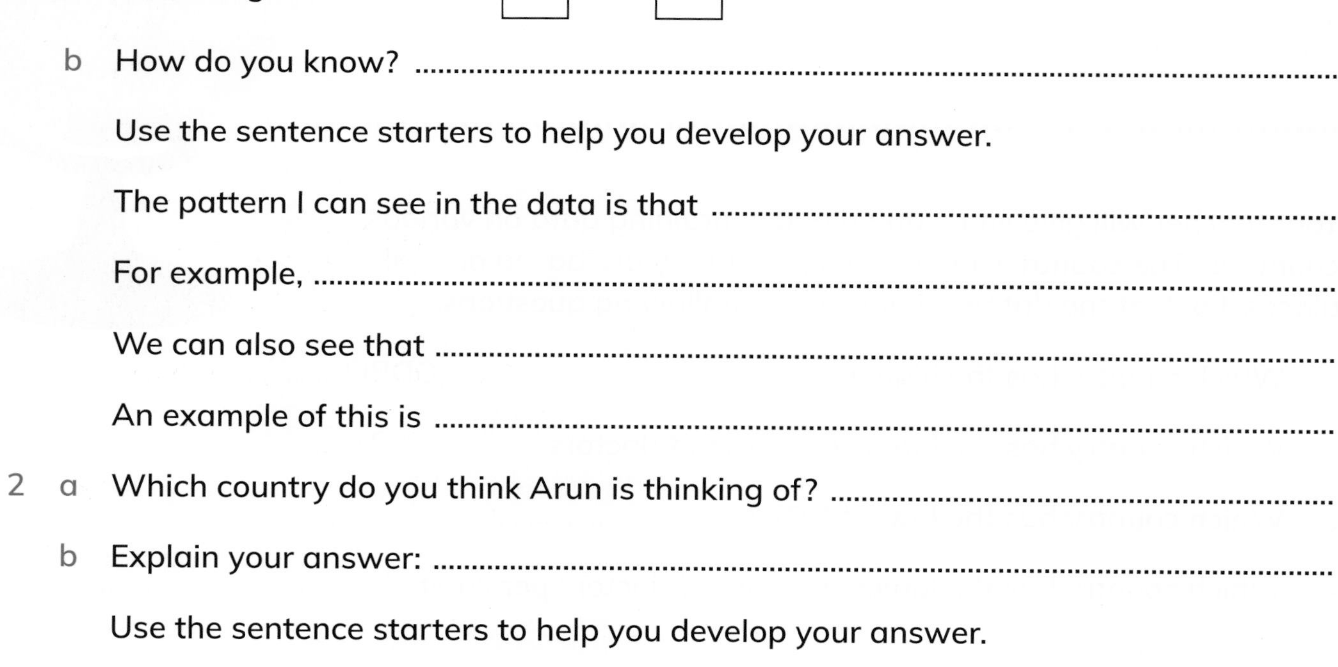

2 a Which country do you think Arun is thinking of? ....

b Explain your answer: ....

Use the sentence starters to help you develop your answer.

The country I think Arun is talking about is ....

The pattern I can see in the data is that ....

However, we can see that ....

....

Peer feedback

Talk about your work with a partner. Listen to what they say about their work and then ask them to tell you the answers to these questions:

1 Have you identified useful data when you answered your questions? YES/NO

2 Can you explain how different people might think or believe different things about this topic? YES/NO

Class discussion

Make some notes on the following in preparation for a class discussion.

1 a If you had to choose one of the countries on the chart to live in, which one would it be?

....

b Explain your answer: ....

2 a What other data might help you to make a decision? ....

b Explain your answer: ....

Share your ideas with a partner.

3 a If your partner had to choose one of the countries on the chart to live in, which one would it be? ....

b Explain their answer: ....

4 a What other data might help them to make a decision? ....

b Explain their answer: ....

Be ready to discuss your ideas and your partner's ideas in class.

Then reflect on the following:

In this lesson, you have considered how different countries make use of unequal resources:

- What did you learn about how different groups made use of unequal resources in Lesson 2?
- What did you learn about how different countries make use of unequal resources in this lesson?

Independent reflection activity

Check your learning goals

If you are sure you have met them and can give a reason why put a '★'.

If you think you have met them put a '☺'.

If you think you are not quite there yet put a '😐'.

Self-assessment Lessons 4–6

How will I know if I have achieved my learning goals?

Use this activity to reflect on how well you have progressed over the last three lessons.

Tick (✓) 'Achieved' if you are sure you have made good progress with this skill and can give an example.

Tick (✓) 'Not there yet / with help' if you need some further practice so that you can make more progress.

If you tick 'Achieved', then challenge yourself to make further progress in the next section.

If you tick 'Not there yet / with help', there will be the chance to consolidate this skill in future lessons.

Continued

Analysis learning objectives To develop my knowledge and understanding about:	Not there yet / with help	Achieved	Example
identifying perspectives			
interpreting data			
making connections			
solving problems			

Reflect on your responses in your self-assessment and identify one area for improvement.

One area I want to improve in is:

....

How I will improve:

....

Challenge topic review

Think about the Challenge topic you have been exploring and complete the following statements.

I was surprised to discover/explore that ....

....

I did not know ....

....

I now think ....

....

Getting better at analysis skills: Lesson 7

Analysis learning objectives

2.1 Identifying perspectives

2.2 Interpreting data

Lesson learning goals

These are the goals for this lesson.
You will return to this table at the end of the lesson for the independent reflection activity.

My learning goals To get better at:	I think	My teacher/ partner thinks
explaining why people think or believe different things about a topic		
using data in graphs or charts to reach a simple conclusion		

Prior learning

Why do people visit parks in cities? Decide which of these reasons you think is the most important and give each a number from 1 (most important) to 5 (least important).

Reason for visiting parks	Number (1–5)
• To meet friends	
• To get some fresh air	
• To relax	
• To look at nature	
• To get some exercise	

Explain your answers to a partner. Do you both agree?
Can you think of other reasons why people visit parks in cities?
Why do you like visiting parks?

Starter activity

The topic I am working on today is:

....

Marcus and his friends have two big parks near them in their city – Green Park and City Park. Marcus tells his friends about some news he heard on the radio. Read what they say and then think about your answers to the questions for class discussion.

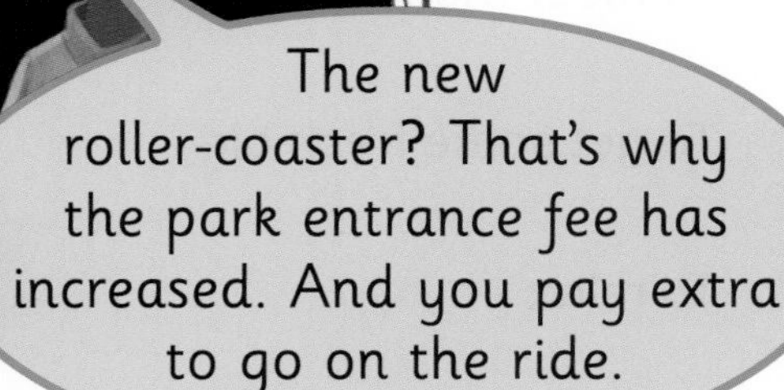

Class discussion

1 Some people think that parks in cities should be open to everyone, free of charge. Do you agree? Give your reasons.

2 Elderly people and young people might have different reasons for visiting a park. How can parks be made attractive to people of all ages?

Main activity

Green Park has published some data showing how many people on average visit the park each week. Look at the chart, and then answer the questions.

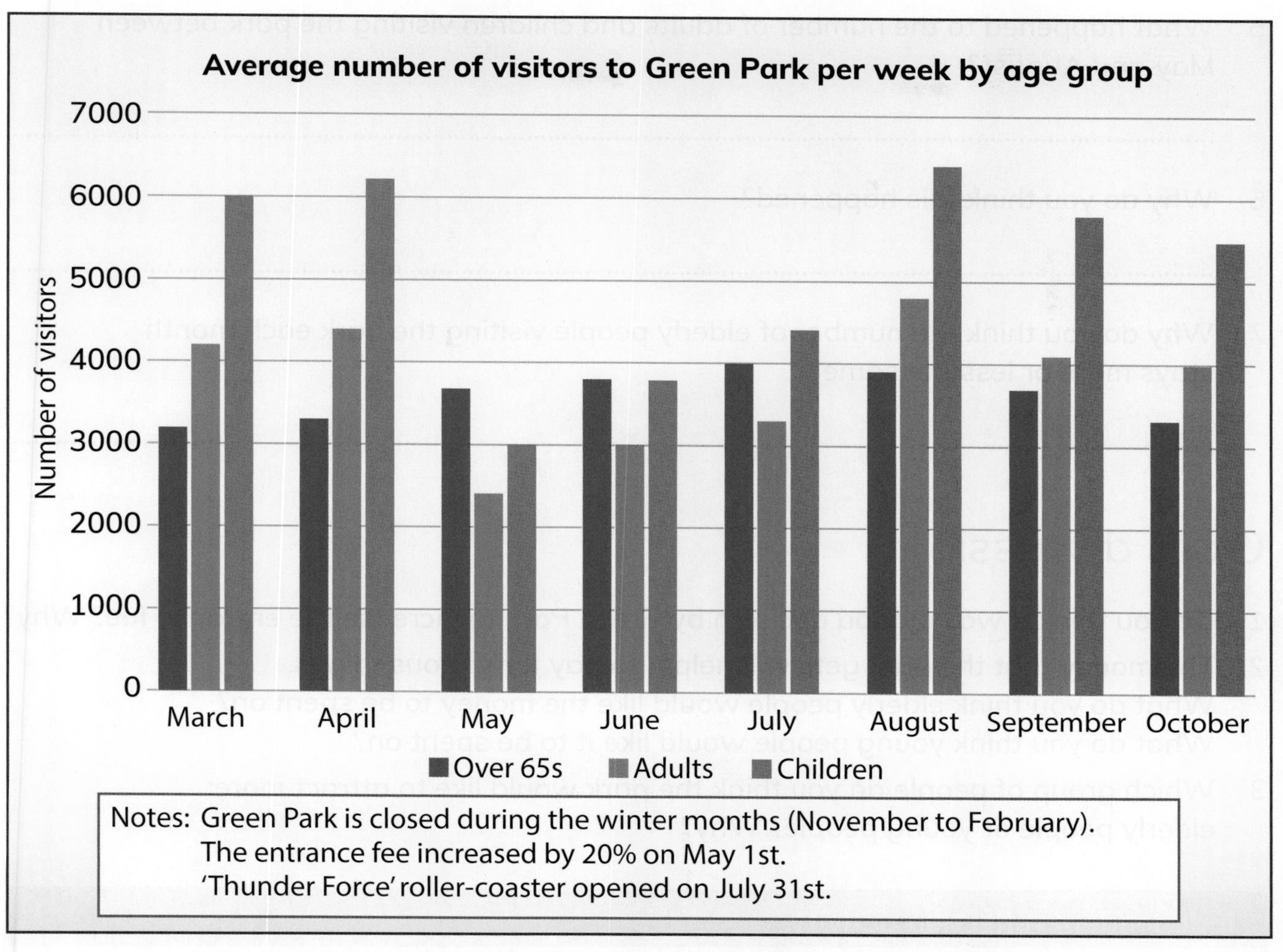

1 In which month did fewest adults and children visit the park? ....

2 Why do you think this happened?

....

3 In which month did most adults and children visit the park? ....

4 Why do you think this happened?

....

5 What happened to the number of adults and children visiting the park between May and August?

....

6 Why do you think this happened?

....

7 Why do you think the number of elderly people visiting the park each month stays more or less the same?

....

Class discussion

1 Do you think it was a good decision by Green Park to increase the entrance fee? Why?

2 The money that the park gets will help it to pay for various things.
What do you think elderly people would like the money to be spent on?
What do you think young people would like it to be spent on?

3 Which group of people do you think the park would like to attract more: elderly people or young people? Why?

Independent reflection activity

Check your learning goals

If you are sure you have met them and can give a reason why put a '★'.

If you think you have met them put a '☺'.

If you think you are not quite there yet put a '😐'.

8

Getting better at analysis skills: Lesson 8

Analysis learning objectives

2.1 Identifying perspectives

2.3 Making connections

Lesson learning goals

These are the goals for this lesson.
You will return to this table at the end of the lesson for the independent reflection activity.

My learning goals To get better at:	I think	My teacher/ partner thinks
explaining why people think or believe different things about a topic		
discussing why other people do things, and how their actions affect others		

Prior learning

A park in Marcus's city needs to save money. Here are some ways that the park could do this. Put them in order from 1 (would least affect people who visit the park) to 6 (would most affect people who visit the park).

Way of saving money	Number (1–6)
• Reducing the number of hours the park is open each day	☐
• Turning off water fountains	☐
• Paying fewer workers to pick up litter and keep the park clean	☐
• Closing the park during the winter	☐
• Removing playground equipment for children to play on	☐
• Cancelling events like open-air concerts and sports competitions	☐

Talk to a partner. Explain your answers. What else could the park do to save money?

Starter activity

The topic I am working on today is:

....

Marcus and his friends are discussing what they'd like to do at the weekend. Read what they say, and think of how Marcus could persuade his friends to go to a park with him.

Marcus reads a guide to the two parks in his city. Your teacher will give you a download showing part of each guide. Work with a partner. Your partner has a different worksheet with the information that is missing from your part of the guide. Exchange the information with your partner to complete the guide.

Class discussion

1 What reasons could there be for people choosing to visit City Park instead of Green Park? Why might people choose to visit Green Park instead of City Park?

2 Which of the two parks do you think Marcus might persuade his friends to visit this weekend? Why?

Main activity

Marcus reads this news in a local newspaper.

City Park to close!

Leaders of the city council say that City Park may have to close because of a shortage of money. The park, which is the only green space in the Central District, is free to the public but costs the city millions of dollars every year …

Think of two people who would react differently to the news because it affects them in different ways.

- Who are the people?
- Is their reaction to the news positive or negative?
- Why do they feel this way?
- What will they do now?

Complete the table below, imagining what the two people might say. An example has been done for you.

Person	Reaction 🙂 🙁	Reason	Action
Local tax-payer	🙂	We tax-payers pay our money to the city to keep the park open while other people use it for free!	I'm going to write to the city council telling them to use the land to make a profit so that we can pay less tax.

Peer feedback

Show your work to a partner. Ask them to answer 'Yes' or 'No' to these statements about your work:

1 I've thought of people who are affected in different ways by the park closing. YES/NO

2 I've thought of good reasons for the way they feel about this. YES/NO

If the answer to either statement is 'No', what changes could you make?

....

Independent reflection activity

Check your learning goals

If you are sure you have met them and can give a reason why put a '★'.

If you think you have met them put a '☺'.

If you think you are not quite there yet put a '😐'.

Getting better at analysis skills: Lesson 9

Analysis learning objectives

2.3 Making connections

2.4 Solving problems

Lesson learning goals

These are the goals for this lesson.
You will return to this table at the end of the lesson for the independent reflection activity.

My learning goals To get better at:	I think	My teacher/ partner thinks
discussing why other people do things, and how their actions affect others		
deciding the most effective action I could take to make a difference to a local issue		

Prior learning

Marcus has made an acrostic using the letters of the word 'parks'. He adds a word or phrase beginning with those letters that come to mind when he thinks of parks. What comes to your mind when you think of parks? Make your own acrostic!

P	picnics	P	
A	air clean enough to breathe	A	
R	riding bicycles	R	
K	kite-flying	K	
S	sunbathing	S	

Talk with a partner. Explain why you have chosen the words and phrases in your acrostic. What other words and phrases could you add to your acrostic?

Starter activity

The topic I am working on today is:

....

Following the news that City Park might close, Marcus sees this poster on the school noticeboard.

Read the poster and then think about your answers to the questions for class discussion.

Class discussion

1 Who are the people who might join this campaign? Why?
2 What actions could people take to save the park?
3 How might these actions affect other people?

Main activity

Marcus and his friends decide to join the campaign to save City Park. They discuss what action they could take.

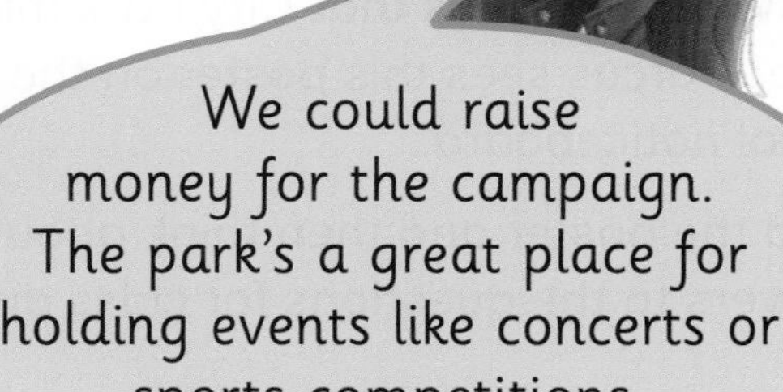

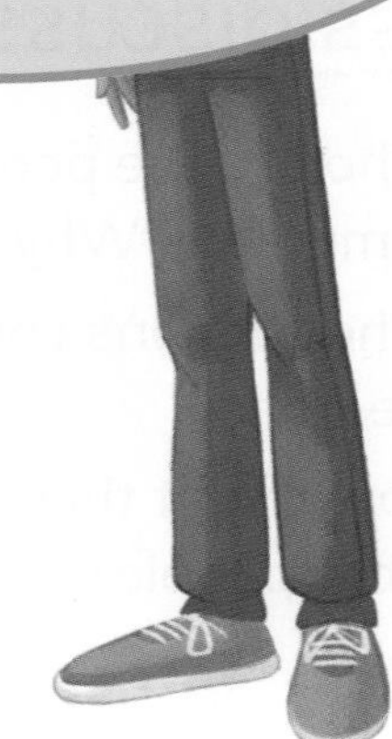

Which of their actions do you think would be the most effective?
Working together in a group or as a pair, plan an action to help save the park.

Our action	Who will be involved	What we hope to achieve

Class discussion

Report your group's action to the class, explaining who will be involved and what you hope to achieve. Respond to questions from others. Listen to what others tell you about their actions. Ask questions to find out more.

Independent reflection activity

Check your learning goals

If you are sure you have met them and can give a reason why put a '★'.

If you think you have met them put a '☺'.

If you think you are not quite there yet put a '😐'.

Self-assessment Lessons 7–9

How will I know if I have achieved my learning goals?

Use this activity to reflect on how well you have progressed over the last three lessons.

Tick (✓) 'Achieved' if you are sure you have made good progress with this skill and can give an example.

Tick (✓) 'Not there yet / with help' if you need some further practice so that you can make more progress.

If you tick 'Achieved', then challenge yourself to make further progress in the next section.

If you tick 'Not there yet / with help', there will be the chance to consolidate this skill in future lessons.

Continued

Analysis learning objectives To get better at:	Not there yet / with help	Achieved	Example
identifying perspectives			
interpreting data			
making connections			
solving problems			

Reflect on your responses in your self-assessment and identify one area for improvement.

One area I want to improve in is:

....

How I will improve:

....

Challenge topic review

Think about the Challenge topic you have been exploring and complete the following statements.

I was surprised to discover/explore that ....

....

I did not know ....

....

I now think ....

....

Starting with evaluation skills: Lesson 1

Evaluation learning objectives

3.1 Evaluating sources

3.2 Evaluating arguments

Lesson learning goals

These are the goals for this lesson.
You will return to this table at the end of the lesson for the independent reflection activity.

My learning goals To start to:	I think	My teacher/ partner thinks
talk about a source and how it is relevant to a topic		
give reasons for my opinion about a topic		

Zara is reading an advertisement for a school. Look at the advertisement and consider what is fact and what is opinion. Underline facts in one colour and opinions in a different colour.

The path to success begins at

The Excel Academy International school

The Excel Academy International School (established 2013) offers top-quality education that gives all children the best start in life. Our school motto is 'Every child a winner'. With our team of 35 highly-trained teachers, your child is sure to succeed!

Talk with a partner. Tell each other some facts about your own school.

Starter activity

The topic I am working on today is:

....

Sofia's class are doing a project about schools and education in different countries around the world. They think of some questions that they would like to know the answers to. Read the questions and then think about what you will say in the class discussion.

a How old are children when they start school?
b At what age are children allowed to leave school?
c How much time do children spend at school each week?
d What time does the school day begin and end?

Class discussion

1 What are the answers to these questions in your country?
2 Should changes be made to schools and education in your country, in your opinion? Give reasons explaining why you think this.

Main activity

Sofia's group decide to find answers to the questions in the Starter activity by doing some research about another country's education system. They find some sources. Look at the sources that your teacher will give you. You will see the title and just the first few sentences of each source. Which of the questions will each source help Sofia to answer?

Write the title of each of your sources in the table below, and then tick (✓) the letter of the question that it will give answers to. Be careful – one of your sources is not relevant to any of the questions!

Title of source	Question: a	b	c	d	Not relevant

Work with a partner. Your partner will help you to complete the table by telling you about their sources.

Class discussion

1 Explain how you knew which question (a–d) each source was relevant to.

2 What other questions could you answer using the two sources that were not relevant?

3 Which of the sources do you find most interesting? Why?

Independent reflection activity

Check your learning goals

If you are sure you have met them and can give a reason why put a '★'.

If you think you have met them put a '☺'.

If you think you are not quite there yet put a '😐'.

Starting with evaluation skills: Lesson 2

Evaluation learning objectives

3.1 Evaluating sources

3.2 Evaluating arguments

Lesson learning goals

These are the goals for this lesson.
You will return to this table at the end of the lesson for the independent reflection activity.

My learning goals To start to:	I think	My teacher/ partner thinks
talk about a source and how it is relevant to a topic		
give reasons for my opinion about a topic		

Prior learning

Marcus is doing some research about class size. He searches online to find out if classes in other countries are bigger or smaller than in his country. Which of these search results would be most useful to him?

1

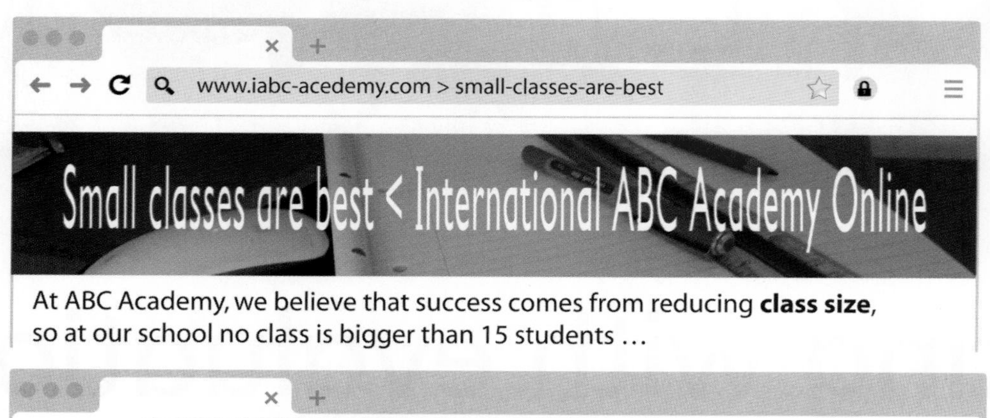

2

www.teachertalk2teacher.com > 2019/07/08 > class-size-debate

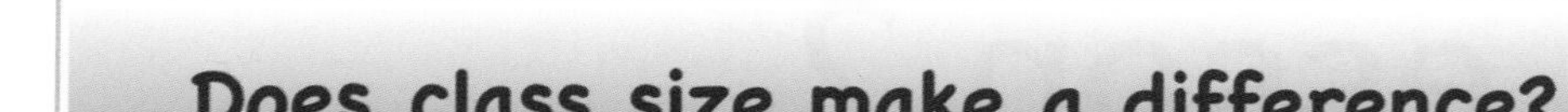

TeacherTalk2Teacher

Around the world, most teachers believe that the smaller the **class size**, the better the chance of all students achieving success. But is this true? At our school …

3

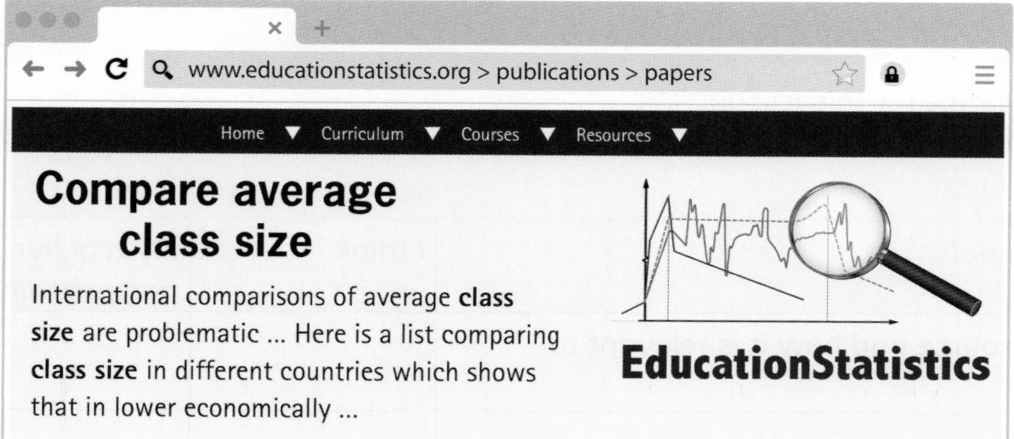

Talk to a partner. How did you decide which website would be most useful for Marcus?

Starter activity

The topic I am working on today is:

....

Sofia's group think of a question about schools and education that they would like to do more research into. Before they begin their research, they make a mind-map to help them organise their ideas. Look at the mind-map and think about your answers to the questions for class discussion.

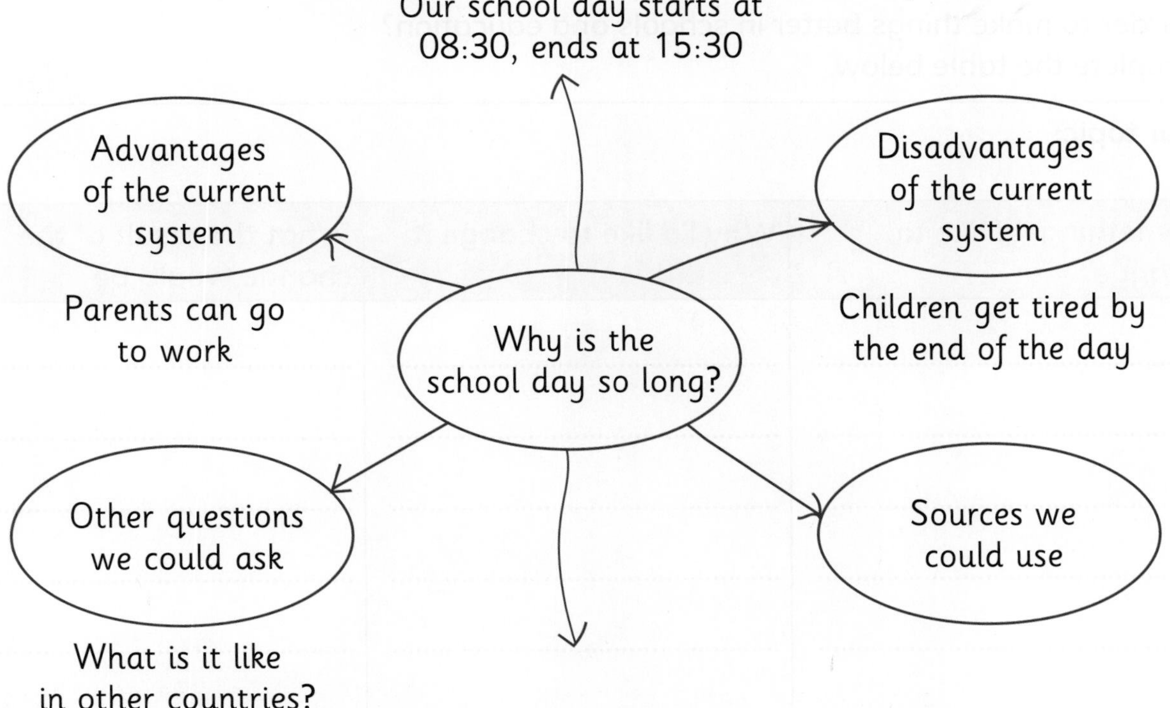

Class discussion

1 What sources could Sofia's group use to find out more?
2 What other advantages and disadvantages can you think of?
3 What other questions could be asked?

Main activity

1 Work in a group. Choose a topic about schools and education in your country that you would like to find out more about and think of a question to ask. You can choose one of the questions (a–d) from the Starter activity in Lesson 1, if you like or make up your own. Use the download that your teacher gives you to make your own mind-map.

2 Look at your mind-map. In your opinion, what needs to change about the topic you have chosen in order to make things better in schools and education? Complete the table below.

Our topic:		
Something I'd like to change	**Why I'd like to change it**	**What the result of the change would be**
....	....	....
....	....	....
....	....	....
....	....	....
....	....	....
....	....	....

Peer feedback

Show your work to a partner from a different group.
Ask them to answer 'Yes' or 'No' to these statements:

1 I have listed some useful sources on my mind-map. YES/NO

2 I have given a good reason why I would like to change something. YES/NO

If the answer to either statement is 'No', what changes could you make?
(Write what your partner tells you here):

....

Independent reflection activity

Check your learning goals

If you are sure you have met them and can give a reason why put a '★'.

If you think you have met them put a '☺'.

If you think you are not quite there yet put a '😐'.

Self-assessment Lessons 1–2

How will I know if I have achieved my learning goals?

Use this activity to reflect on how well you have progressed over the last two lessons.

Tick (✓) 'Achieved' if you are sure you have made good progress with this skill and can give an example.

Tick (✓) 'Not there yet / with help' if you need some further practice so that you can make more progress.

If you tick 'Achieved', then challenge yourself to make further progress in the next section.

If you tick 'Not there yet / with help', there will be the chance to consolidate this skill in future lessons.

Continued

Evaluation learning objectives To start to:	Not there yet / with help	Achieved	Example
evaluate sources			
evaluate arguments			

Reflect on your responses in your self-assessment and identify one area for improvement.

One area I want to improve in is:

....

How I will improve:

....

Challenge topic review

Think about the Challenge topic you have been exploring and complete the following statements.

I was surprised to discover/explore that ....

....

I did not know ....

....

I now think ....

....

Developing evaluation skills: Lesson 3

Evaluation learning objectives

3.1 Evaluating sources

3.2 Evaluating arguments

Lesson learning goals

These are the goals for this lesson.
You will return to this table at the end of the lesson for the independent reflection activity.

My learning goals To develop my knowledge and understanding about:	I think	My teacher/ partner thinks
how to talk about a source and its relevance to a topic and the author's viewpoint		
how to give reasons for my opinion about a topic		

Prior learning

Zara is doing a research project about computers in education. She goes to the library and finds three books with 'education' in the title. She reads the blurb about each book. Read the blurbs below and decide, from this information, which book you think will be most useful to her.

A After a successful career as a teacher, Aisha Bernhardt has written an autobiographical account of her years in the classroom. She shares her experiences of teaching students around the world and her views on the future of education.

B Dr Julio Miyake teaches at the School of Education in Artsville, where he also carries out research on teaching and learning in the classroom. In his latest book, he explains the impact of new technology on schools and education in general.

C Award-winning journalist Ed Fontana has written about many different subjects, including fishing, computer games and healthy eating. In this book, he discusses how schools should educate young people about the environment.

Talk to a partner. How did you decide which book would be most useful for Zara's research project?

Starter activity

The topic I am working on today is:

....

At Arun's school, builders are constructing some new classrooms. While this is happening, half the school is closed. Students can only attend lessons at school for two days a week. For the rest of the time, they must study at home. Read what Arun and his friends say about this, and then discuss your answers to the questions.

Class discussion

Imagine that your school is in the same situation as Arun's school.

1 What would you like about studying at home instead of at school? Give your reasons.

2 What wouldn't you like? Why?

3 How could the school help you to study at home?

Main activity

Arun's parents are looking for ways that they could help Arun to study at home. They have found some sources – your teacher will give you these.
Read the brief excerpts from each of the sources.
Which of them would be useful for Arun's parents?
One example has been done for you.

	Source Title	Useful	Not useful
A	Newspaper report 'Home or School? Choosing the best for your child'	✓	
B	learnmaths@home.com website		
C	Advertisement for Global Internet Academy		
D	greenworldleisurecentres.com website		
E	Advertisement for Excellence Home Tutoring		
F	zenithinternationalacademy.com website		

Look again at each of the sources. Each of them contains some facts and some opinions. In each source, underline or highlight one piece of factual information in one colour, and underline or highlight one opinion in a different colour.

Class discussion

1 Which of the sources do you think Arun's parents would find most useful? Give your reasons.
2 What other sources do you think would be useful for Arun's parents?

Independent reflection activity

Check your learning goals

If you are sure you have met them and can give a reason why put a '★'.

If you think you have met them put a '☺'.

If you think you are not quite there yet put a '😐'.

Developing evaluation skills: Lesson 4

Evaluation learning objectives

3.1 Evaluating sources

3.2 Evaluating arguments

Lesson learning goals

These are the goals for this lesson.
You will return to this table at the end of the lesson for the independent reflection activity.

My learning goals To develop my knowledge and understanding about:	I think	My teacher/ partner thinks
how to explain my opinion of another person's viewpoint		

Prior learning

Arun's school is thinking of having a school uniform that all the students must wear. Which of these people might be **for** the idea, and which might be **against**? Put a tick (✓) if they are 'for' and a cross (✗) if they are 'against'. One example has been done for you.

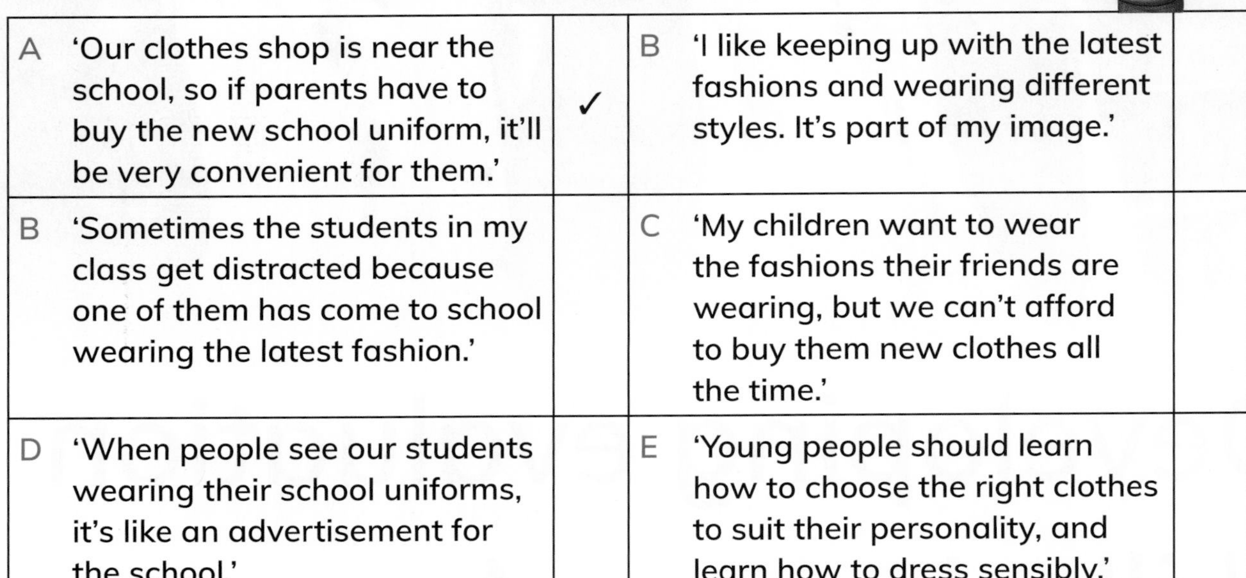

A 'Our clothes shop is near the school, so if parents have to buy the new school uniform, it'll be very convenient for them.'	✓	B 'I like keeping up with the latest fashions and wearing different styles. It's part of my image.'	
B 'Sometimes the students in my class get distracted because one of them has come to school wearing the latest fashion.'		C 'My children want to wear the fashions their friends are wearing, but we can't afford to buy them new clothes all the time.'	
D 'When people see our students wearing their school uniforms, it's like an advertisement for the school.'		E 'Young people should learn how to choose the right clothes to suit their personality, and learn how to dress sensibly.'	

Talk to a partner. Who could each of these people be?

Starter activity

The topic I am working on today is:

....

While building work is continuing, Arun's school has asked students to come to school for only two days a week, and to spend the rest of the time studying at home. Some parents have responded to this decision by writing to the school. Read a letter from one parent that your teacher gives you.

Now work with a partner.

Your partner has read a letter from a different parent.
Discuss with your partner the answers to the questions for class discussion below.

Class discussion

1 What is the opinion of each of the letter writers about the school's decision?
2 What do you think the main reason is for the writer's bias for or against the school's decision?
3 What evidence of the writer's bias is there in each letter?
4 How do you think the school should respond to each of the letters?

Main activity

Work with a partner. Look again at both letters (A and B) and complete the table in the download that your teacher will give you.

Peer feedback

Show your work to a different partner and ask them to answer 'Yes' or 'No' to these statements:

1 It is clear what I agree or disagree with the letter writers about. YES/NO
2 I've given good reasons for agreeing or disagreeing with the letter writers. YES/NO

If the answer to either of the statements is 'NO', what changes could you make? (Write what they tell you here):

....

Independent reflection activity

Check your learning goals

If you are sure you have met them and can give a reason why put a '★'.

If you think you have met them put a '☺'.

If you think you are not quite there yet put a '😐'.

Self-assessment Lessons 3–4

How will I know if I have achieved my learning goals?

Use this activity to reflect on how well you have progressed over the last two lessons.

Tick (✓) 'Achieved' if you are sure you have made good progress with this skill and can give an example.

Tick (✓) 'Not there yet / with help' if you need some further practice so that you can make more progress.

If you tick 'Achieved', then challenge yourself to make further progress in the next section.

If you tick 'Not there yet / with help', there will be the chance to consolidate this skill in future lessons.

Evaluation learning objectives To develop my knowledge and understanding about:	Not there yet / with help	Achieved	Example
evaluating sources			
evaluating arguments			

Reflect on your responses in your self-assessment and identify one area for improvement.

One area I want to improve in is:

....

How I will improve:

....

Challenge topic review

Think about the Challenge topic you have been exploring and complete the following statements.

I was surprised to discover/explore that ....

....

I did not know ....

....

I now think ....

....

Getting better at evaluation skills: Lesson 5

Evaluation learning objectives

3.1 Evaluating sources

3.2 Evaluating arguments

Lesson learning goals

These are the goals for this lesson.
You will return to this table at the end of the lesson for the independent reflection activity.

My learning goals To get better at:	I think	My teacher/ partner thinks
talking about the source and some strengths and limitations of the author's viewpoint		
giving my opinion about a source by talking about its features and arguments		

Prior learning

Sofia has been asked to put together some advice for younger children who are learning to consider sources.

Is she giving good advice?

Explain your answer to a partner.

A biased source is never useful for your research.

Starter activity

The topic I am working on today is:

....

The group have been discussing one of the letters about home learning. They have been asked to:

- identify some strengths of the author's viewpoint
- identify some limitations of the author's viewpoint
- give their opinion about the source by talking about its features
- give their opinion about the source by talking about its arguments.

Exclamation marks are used three times. I think that's too many in a short piece. What are they for?

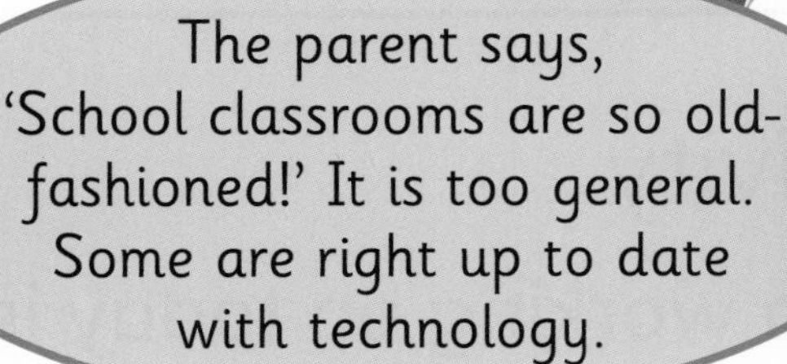

I like the way that when it considers the advantages of technology it considers the impact on different people.

Can you put their views into the table that your teacher gives you? The first one has been done for you. You can use some in more than one place.

Main activity

Find two sources relevant to a topic you are working on, or use the sources provided by your teacher. Discuss them in your group and:

- identify some strengths of each author's viewpoint
- identify some limitations of each author's viewpoint
- give an opinion about each source by talking about its features
- give an opinion about each by talking about its arguments.

Summarise your discussions in the table that your teacher will give you.

Which source do you think is more trustworthy? Why?

Source ....

because ....

Class discussion

Report to the class on the source you have chosen and why.

Independent reflection activity

Check your learning goals

If you are sure you have met them and can give a reason why put a '★'.

If you think you have met them put a '☺'.

If you think you are not quite there yet put a '😐'.

Self-assessment Lesson 5

How will I know if I have achieved my learning goals?

Use this activity to reflect on how well you have progressed over the last lesson.

Tick (✓) 'Achieved' if you are sure you have made good progress with this skill and can give an example.

Tick (✓) 'Not there yet / with help' if you need some further practice so that you can make more progress.

If you tick 'Achieved', then challenge yourself to make further progress in the next section.

If you tick 'Not there yet / with help', there will be the chance to consolidate this skill in future lessons.

Evaluation learning objectives To get better at:	Not there yet / with help	Achieved	Example
evaluating sources			
evaluating arguments			

Continued

Reflect on your responses in your self-assessment and identify one area for improvement.

One area I want to improve in is:

....

How I will improve:

....

Challenge topic review

Think about the Challenge topic you have been exploring and complete the following statements.

I was surprised to discover/explore that ....

....

I did not know ....

....

I now think ....

....

Starting with reflection skills: Lesson 1

Reflection learning objectives

4.1 Personal contribution

Lesson learning goals

These are the goals for this lesson.
You will return to this table at the end of the lesson for the independent reflection activity.

My learning goals To start to:	I think	My teacher/ partner thinks
describe something good about my work as a member of a team, and/or something that I need to improve		

Prior learning

What do you think good teamwork looks like?

On a piece of A4 paper, draw one or more pictures to show your ideas.

Talk to a partner. Explain what your pictures show about good teamwork. Listen to what your partner tells you about their pictures. Do you agree?

Starter activity

The topic I am working on today is:

....

Zara and her team-mates are going on a school trip to a foreign country to see how the lives of children there are different to their own. As part of their trip, they'll visit a school. Before they leave, they talk about some of the things they would like to find out about schools in another country.

Read what they say and then think of two more questions about schools in other countries that you would like to ask.

It'll be interesting to see whether children there study the same subjects at school as we do, or something different.

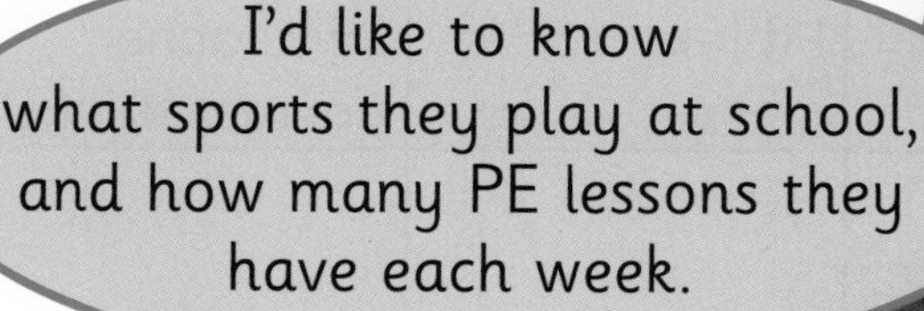

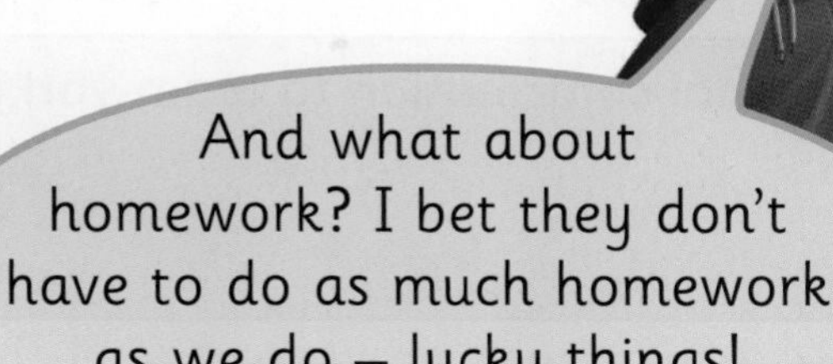

My questions:

a ....

b ....

Class discussion

1 What differences would you expect to find between schools in your country and schools in other countries?

2 What do you think would be the same?

Main activity

Work in a group. With the others in your group, decide the four most interesting questions to ask about schools in other countries.

Questions we'd like to ask:

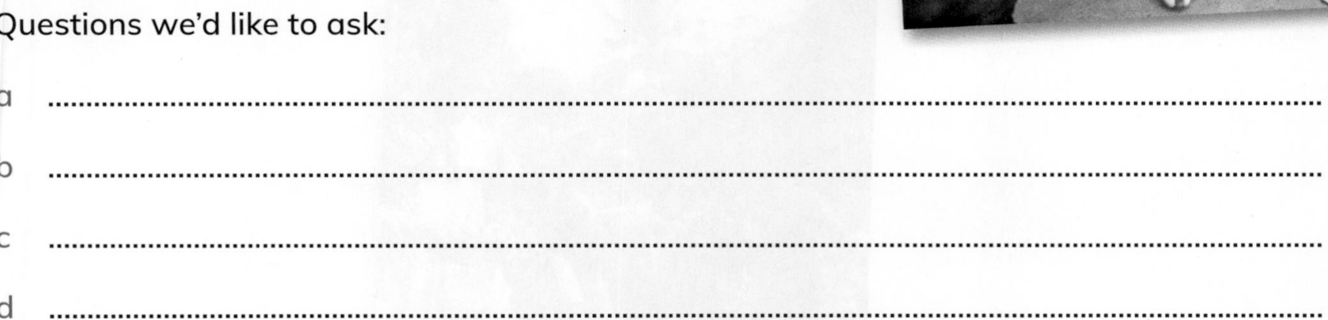

a ....

b ....

c ....

d ....

Peer feedback

Ask a partner from your group to give you a score for each of the ways that you helped your team to complete the task in the Main activity:

My personal contribution to teamwork	Agree ☺		☹︎ neutral 😐		Disagree ☹
	5	4	3	2	1
a I listened to others in my team.					
b I made some helpful suggestions.					
c I kept my focus on the task.					
d I helped my team to agree.					
Other . . .					

What would you like to improve next time you work in a team?

....

Independent reflection activity

Check your learning goals

If you are sure you have met them and can give a reason why put a '★'.

If you think you have met them put a '☺'.

If you think you are not quite there yet put a '😐'.

Starting with reflection skills: Lesson 2

Reflection learning objectives

4.2 Teamwork

Lesson learning goals

These are the goals for this lesson.
You will return to this table at the end of the lesson for the independent reflection activity.

My learning goals To start to:	I think	My teacher/ partner thinks
talk about how working as a team helps us to achieve our goal		

Prior learning

Sofia has chosen three numbers to present some data about her school. Match the numbers to the reasons she gives for choosing them.

		Number
1	This is the number of teachers at our school.	
2	This is the age of the oldest students at our school.	
3	This is how many hours we spend at school each day.	

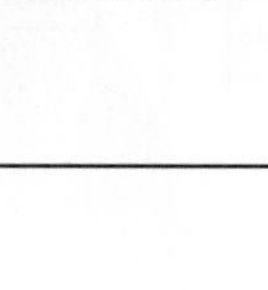

Now choose three numbers to present some data about your school. Write them here:

Talk with a partner. Can they guess what the numbers mean? What do you think your partner's numbers mean?

Starter activity

The topic I am working on today is:

....

Students in another country have asked Arun and his classmates to send them some information about their school. Read the questions they have sent, and then think about what you will say in the class discussion.

1 How old is your school?	2 What is the maximum class size?	3 How many students are there at your school?	4 How many teachers are there?
5 How many other adults work at your school?	6 What are the ages of the students at your school?	7 How many computers (PCs, laptops, tablets, etc.) does your school have?	8 How many PE lessons a week does each class have?
9 What after-school activities for students are there at your school?	10 How do most students travel to your school every day?	11 How many classrooms does your school have?	12 How many subjects do you have to study at your school?
13 Are there the same number of boys and girls at your school?	14 Are there equal numbers of male and female teachers?	15 How many hours of lessons do you have each week?	16 How long are your school holidays every year?

Class discussion

Imagine that someone asked you these questions about your school.

1 Which of the questions do you know the answers to?

2 How could you find the information for the questions you do not know the answers to?

Main activity

Work in a group. Your group has been given the task of finding the answers to Questions 1–16 about your school so that the information can be sent to students at a school in another country.

What information do you need to find out about your school? How will you find out this information? In your group, who will do what?

Make a plan to show how your group will complete this task.
Use the headings below, and write your plan in the download that your teacher will give you, or copy it onto your own paper.

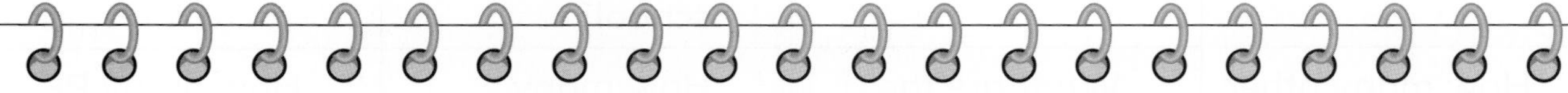

What we need to find out	How we will find it out	Who in the group will do it

Class discussion

1 How will working as a team help your group to complete the task?
2 What do you think the challenges of working as a group might be?

Independent reflection activity

Check your learning goals

If you are sure you have met them and can give a reason why put a '★'.

If you think you have met them put a '☺'.

If you think you are not quite there yet put a '😐'.

Starting with reflection skills: Lesson 3

Reflection learning objectives

4.3 Personal viewpoints

4.4 Personal learning

Lesson learning goals

These are the goals for this lesson.
You will return to this table at the end of the lesson for the independent reflection activity.

My learning goals To start to:	I think	My teacher/ partner thinks
talk about something that I learnt during an activity		
describe an activity that helped me to learn something		

Prior learning

Sofia and her friends are talking about teamwork. Some of these sentences are about the benefits of working as a team and some are about challenges. Which is which? One example has been done for you.

	Benefit ☺	Challenge 😐
1 Nobody listens to what other team members are saying.		✓
2 As a team, we do more because we share the work.		
3 Other team members can help you to solve problems.		
4 Some people work more slowly than others.		
5 One person might want to do everything on their own.		
6 Each team member can do what they are good at.		

Talk with a partner. How can you solve the challenges of teamwork? What other benefits are there?

Starter activity

The topic I am working on today is:

....

Arun and his classmates have found the answers to the questions they were asked about their school in Lesson 2. Working as a team, share the information in the download that your teacher will give you, and match the answers to Questions 1–16.

Class discussion

What differences are there between your school and Arun's school?

Main activity

Think about the teamwork activities you have done in this lesson, and in Lessons 1 and 2.

Tell your partner which of these things you have improved at when working as a member of a team:

- Listening to my team-mates
- Making helpful suggestions
- Keeping my focus on the task
- Helping my team to agree
- Other

What activities helped you to improve your teamwork most? Why?

What would you still like to improve at?

Listen to what your partner says.
How could you help them to improve at teamwork?

Class discussion

1. What are the benefits of working as a team, in your experience?
2. What are the challenges?

Independent reflection activity

Check your learning goals

If you are sure you have met them and can give a reason why put a '★'.

If you think you have met them put a '☺'.

If you think you are not quite there yet put a '😐'.

Self-assessment Lessons 1–3

How will I know if I have achieved my learning goals?

Use this activity to reflect on how well you have progressed over the last three lessons.

Tick (✓) 'Achieved' if you are sure you have made good progress with this skill and can give an example.

Tick (✓) 'Not there yet / with help' if you need some further practice so that you can make more progress.

If you tick 'Achieved', then challenge yourself to make further progress in the next section.

If you tick 'Not there yet / with help', there will be the chance to consolidate this skill in future lessons.

Reflection learning objectives To start to:	Not there yet / with help	Achieved	Example
reflect on personal contribution			
reflect on teamwork			
reflect on personal viewpoints			
reflect on personal learning			

Reflect on your responses in your self-assessment and identify one area for improvement.

One area I want to improve in is:

....

How I will improve:

....

Challenge topic review

Think about the Challenge topic you have been exploring and complete the following statements.

I was surprised to discover/explore that ....

....

I did not know ....

....

I now think ....

....

4 Developing reflection skills: Lesson 4

Reflection learning objectives

4.1 Personal contribution

4.2 Teamwork

Lesson learning goals

These are the goals for this lesson.
You will return to this table at the end of the lesson for the independent reflection activity.

My learning goals To develop my knowledge and understanding about:	I think	My teacher/ partner thinks
the strengths and/or limitations of my work as a member of a team		
the benefits and/or challenges of working together as a team to achieve our goal		

Prior learning

Imagine that someone from another country has asked you to send them three photos to show them what your school is like. What three photos would you take? You can draw them in these frames or describe them in words if you prefer:

1	2	3

Talk to a partner. From your partner's photos and your own, which three would you choose to send? Why?

Starter activity

The topic I am working on today is:

....

Some students from another country are coming to visit Marcus's school. Marcus and his classmates discuss what they could do to make their visitors feel welcome.

Read what they say, and then think about your answers to the questions in the class discussion.

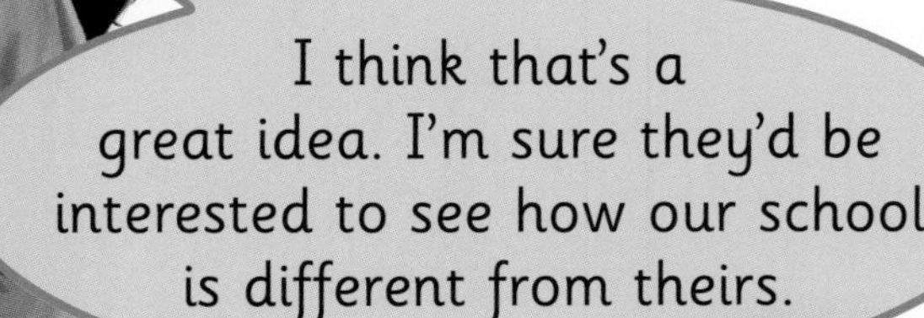

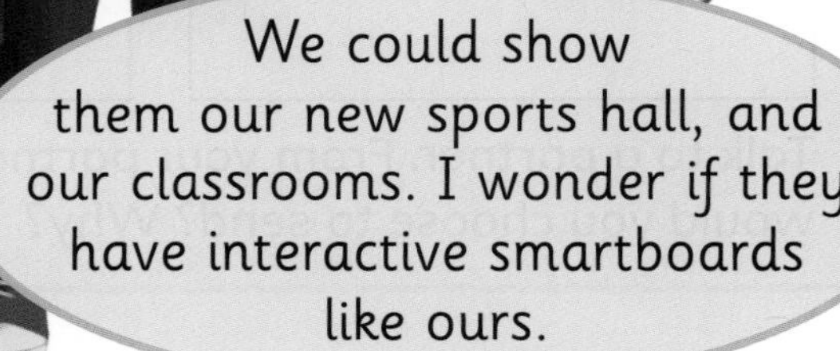

Class discussion

Imagine that some students from another country are going to visit your school.
The students are the same age as you.
It is your job to show the visiting students your school.

1 What would you take the visitors to see in your school? Why?
2 Who do you think the students should meet while they are visiting your school?

Main activity

Work in a group. Plan a tour of your school to show some foreign visitors what it's like. The tour will take place during the school day when other classes will be having lessons.

Decide the starting point for the tour, and plan a route around the school, including all the things that you would like to show them.

Who do you want the visitors to meet on their tour? How long will the tour take? How could you check to see if you have estimated the time correctly?

Peer feedback

Show your group's plan to a partner from another group. Tell them:

- something in the plan that you suggested, and the others in your group agreed to
- something in the plan that others in your group suggested, and you agreed to
- something that you disagreed about with others in your group, and what happened
- something that you think you and your group did well
- something that you think you and your group could have done better.

Now ask your partner to tell you:

Two positive things about the way you worked with others in your group (write what they tell you here):

 ....

★ ....

Something that you could improve the next time you work as a member of a group (write what they tell you here):

 ....

Independent reflection activity

Check your learning goals

If you are sure you have met them and can give a reason why put a '★'.

If you think you have met them put a '☺'.

If you think you are not quite there yet put a '😐'.

5

Developing reflection skills: Lesson 5

Reflection learning objectives

4.1 Personal contribution

4.2 Teamwork

Lesson learning goals

These are the goals for this lesson.
You will return to this table at the end of the lesson for the independent reflection activity.

My learning goals To develop my knowledge and understanding about:	I think	My teacher/ partner thinks
the strengths and/or limitations of my work as a member of a team		
the benefits and/or challenges of working together as a team to achieve our goal		

Prior learning

Arun and his classmates are talking about some problems they have experienced when working as a team.

Problem:	**Who suggests a solution?**
1 Everyone talks at the same time	
2 We always take too long to make a decision	
3 It's hard to agree about who should do what	
4 One team member isn't going to complete their work on time	

Who has a solution? Write their names in the boxes.

Solution:

Arun: Let's decide who has the best skills for each job.

Zara: If we keep checking each other's work, we can offer help if needed.

Marcus: One team member should decide whose turn it is to speak.

Sofia: Why don't we set a time limit to the discussion?

Talk with a partner. What other solutions to the problems can you think of?

Starter activity

The topic I am working on today is:

....

Some students from a foreign country are visiting Marcus's school. Marcus and his classmates have to plan a programme of activities and events for the visitors. They discuss their ideas about the programme.

Read what they say, and then think about your answers to the questions for class discussion.

Class discussion

Imagine that some foreign students are coming to visit your school.

1 What sorts of activities or events would you plan for them?
2 What do you think the visiting students would learn from these activities or events?

Main activity

Work in a group. Plan a programme of activities and events for a group of ten foreign students who are coming to visit your school. Think about:

- How long will the programme be? (Whole-day? Half-day?)
- Timings (How long will each activity or event take? When will each activity or event begin and end? What will the order of activities or events be?)
- Places (Where in your school will each event or activity take place?)
- People (Who will be involved – students, teachers, other?)

You can use these headings for your plan.
Your teacher will give you a full template as a download.

Visit by foreign students			
When?	**Activity or event**	**Where?**	**Who?**

Look at your plan. Imagine that your group is going to put your plan into action. Who in your group would be the best person for each of these roles?

Role	Who would be the best person in our group to do this?
a Invite other people (teachers, students, etc.) to take part in the programme	
b Make sure that everyone knows what to do, and does their job properly	
c Check that everything (equipment, rooms, etc.) is ready before the visit	
d Solve any problems before or during the visit	
e Meet and greet the visitors when they arrive	
f Check that everything happens at the right time during the visit	

Class discussion

Think about the task that your group has just completed.

1 Was it easy or difficult for your group to decide who would do what? Why?
2 How can you make sure that the roles are shared fairly among your group members?
3 What skills do you need to carry out each of the roles?
4 What other roles could there be?

Independent reflection activity

Check your learning goals

If you are sure you have met them and can give a reason why put a '★'.

If you think you have met them put a '☺'.

If you think you are not quite there yet put a '😐'.

Developing reflection skills: Lesson 6

Reflection learning objectives

4.3 Personal viewpoints

4.4 Personal learning

Lesson learning goals

These are the goals for this lesson.
You will return to this table at the end of the lesson for the independent reflection activity.

My learning goals To develop my knowledge and understanding about:	I think	My teacher/ partner thinks
how something I learnt during an activity has changed my way of thinking about a topic		
which activities help me to learn		

Prior learning

Sofia and her classmates are talking about their experiences of working as a team.

Sofia: Everyone had different ideas, so it took us a long time to decide what to do.

Arun: When we were deciding what to do, I kept disagreeing with everyone.

Zara: I suggested that Sofia should design the poster, because she's good at drawing.

Marcus: By sharing the work between us, we achieved our goal on time.

Who talks about:	Name
1 something they did to help the team achieve its goal?	
2 something they could do better next time?	
3 something that is good about working as a team?	
4 something that is difficult about working as a team?	

Talk with a partner. How would you solve the problem that Sofia talks about?

Starter activity

The topic I am working on today is:

....

Before a group of foreign students come to visit their school, Marcus and his classmates have decided to design and make a 'Welcome' banner to hang in the school entrance.

Imagine your group has to carry out this task. Here is a plan showing the steps you could take. Add notes to the plan to show this information by writing in each of the boxes.

Who in your group would do what?

How long would each step take? (Your teacher has given you 45 minutes to complete the whole task of making a banner.)

Plan for making a banner

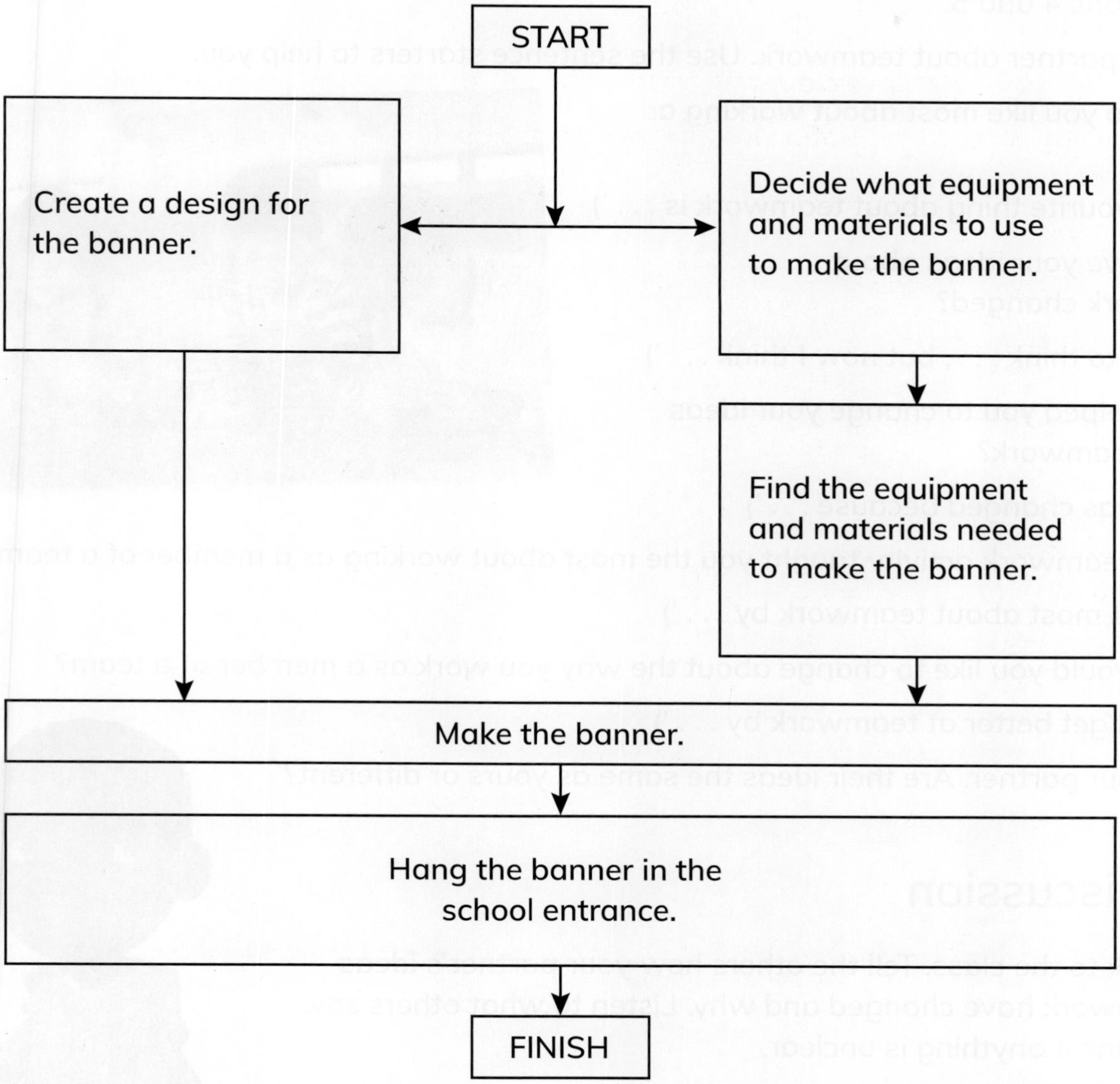

START

Create a design for the banner. | Decide what equipment and materials to use to make the banner.

Find the equipment and materials needed to make the banner.

Make the banner.

Hang the banner in the school entrance.

FINISH

Class discussion

1 What has this activity helped you to learn about working as a team?

2 How has this activity changed your ideas about teamwork?

Main activity

Think about the teamwork activities that you have done in this lesson, and in Lessons 4 and 5.

Talk with a partner about teamwork. Use the sentence starters to help you.

1 What do you like most about working as a team?

('My favourite thing about teamwork is . . . ')

2 How have your ideas about teamwork changed?

('I used to think . . . , but now I think . . . ')

3 What helped you to change your ideas about teamwork?

('My ideas changed because . . . ')

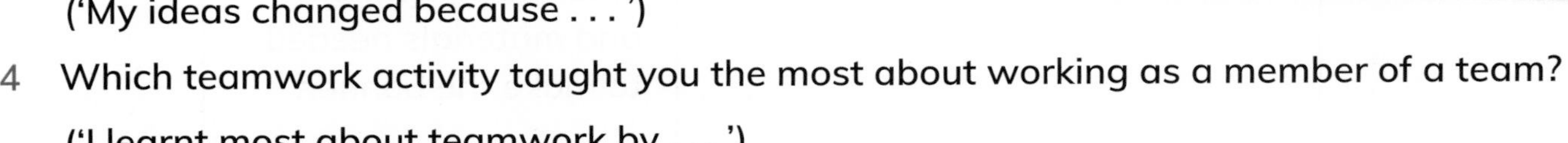

4 Which teamwork activity taught you the most about working as a member of a team?

('I learnt most about teamwork by . . . ')

5 What would you like to change about the way you work as a member of a team?

('I could get better at teamwork by . . . ')

Listen to your partner. Are their ideas the same as yours or different?

Class discussion

Report back to the class. Tell the others how your partner's ideas about teamwork have changed and why. Listen to what others say. Ask questions if anything is unclear.

Independent reflection activity

Check your learning goals

If you are sure you have met them and can give a reason why put a '★'.

If you think you have met them put a '☺'.

If you think you are not quite there yet put a '😐'.

Self-assessment Lessons 4–6

How will I know if I have achieved my learning goals?

Use this activity to reflect on how well you have progressed over the last three lessons.

Tick (✓) 'Achieved' if you are sure you have made good progress with this skill and can give an example.

Tick (✓) 'Not there yet / with help' if you need some further practice so that you can make more progress.

If you tick 'Achieved', then challenge yourself to make further progress in the next section.

If you tick 'Not there yet / with help', there will be the chance to consolidate this skill in future lessons.

Reflection learning objectives To develop my knowledge and understanding about:	Not there yet / with help	Achieved	Example
reflecting on personal contribution			
reflecting on teamwork			
reflecting on personal viewpoints			
reflecting on personal learning			

Reflect on your responses in your self-assessment and identify one area for improvement.

One area I want to improve in is:

....

How I will improve:

....

Challenge topic review

Think about the Challenge topic you have been exploring and complete the following statements.

I was surprised to discover/explore that ....

....

I did not know ....

....

I now think ....

....

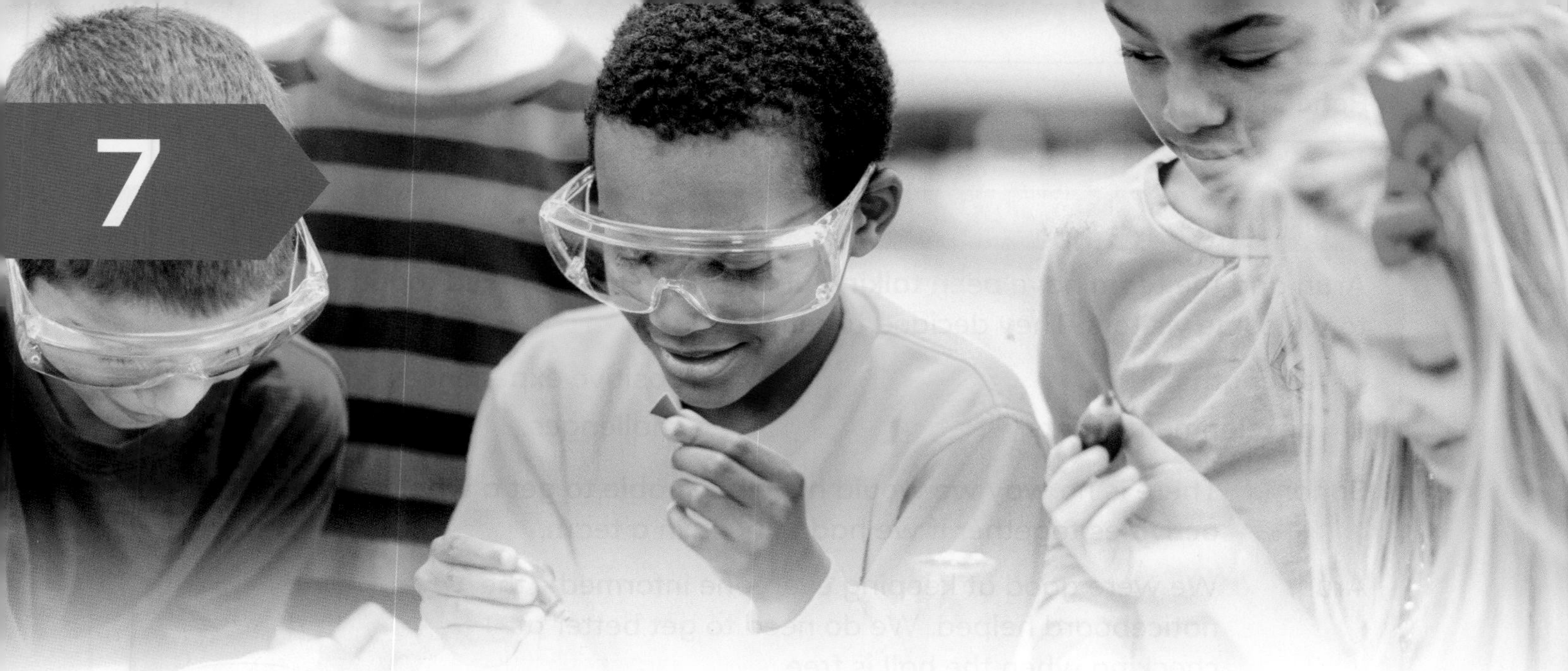

Getting better at reflection skills: Lesson 7

Reflection learning objectives

4.1 Personal contribution

4.2 Teamwork

Lesson learning goals

These are the goals for this lesson.
You will return to this table at the end of the lesson for the independent reflection activity.

My learning goals To get better at:	I think	My teacher/ partner thinks
explaining my strengths and development points when I work as a member of a team		
explaining some of the benefits and challenges of working together as a team		

Prior learning

Arun and the team have been talking about when they worked together to welcome visitors. They decided to reflect on:

- strengths
- development points
- positive experiences
- challenges.

Sofia: There is no way we would have been able to get a whole morning's activities together if we hadn't been in a team.

Arun: We were good at keeping everyone informed – the noticeboard helped. We do need to get better at checking when the hall is free.

Marcus: Agreed – it was tricky to get everyone in the right place at the right time.

Zara: It was great knowing our visitors enjoyed their time with us.

Who said what?

.... discussed strengths.

.... discussed development points.

.... discussed positive experiences.

.... discussed challenges.

Reflect on your group project and then talk to a partner. Prepare your ideas to share in a class discussion.

Starter activity

The topic I am working on today is:

....

Marcus, Sofia, Arun and Zara have been working on a team project for the International Day of Women and Girls in Science on 11 February.

Their school is celebrating the work done by pioneering women in STEM jobs.

The team have taken notes about four pioneering women. Now they want to tell their friends about Valentina Tereshkova, the first woman in space.

Your teacher will give you the notes that the team have taken and a download to create her biography. Can you help them put together their biography of Valentina Tereshkova?

Oh no! All our notes have got completely jumbled up!

Main activity

Reflect on the previous activity and your contribution to the group.

1 What were the strengths of the way your group worked?

2 If you were given the task again, how would you have done it differently?

3 What were the positives of working as part of a team for this task?

4 What were the challenges of working as part of a team for this task?

5 What helps a team work well together?

Class discussion

What is your perspective? Tick (✓) one.

I agree with Arun	I agree with Sofia	I have a different perspective

If you have a different perspective, write it here: ....

....

Explain your reasons for your perspective: ....

....

Independent reflection activity

Check your learning goals

If you are sure you have met them and can give a reason why put a '★'.

If you think you have met them put a '☺'.

If you think you are not quite there yet put a '😐'.

Getting better at reflection skills: Lesson 8

Reflection learning objectives

4.3 Personal viewpoints

4.4 Personal learning

Lesson learning goals

These are the goals for this lesson.
You will return to this table at the end of the lesson for the independent reflection activity.

My learning goals To get better at:	I think	My teacher/ partner thinks
explaining how my ideas about a topic have changed as a result of what I've learnt		
explaining how some activities help me to develop my skills		

Prior learning

The team have been reflecting on a teamwork activity they took part in. Read what each one of them says and think about the answers to the questions.

Zara: Before our team did some reading on this topic, we used to think that there weren't any famous women scientists.

Sofia: Then we found out that 51 women have won the Nobel Prize for STEM work and that Donna Strickland's work in laser physics will help eye surgeons.

Arun: Zara found out that there's this thing called the 'Matilda effect'. It turns out that men have ended up getting the credit for women's discoveries.

Marcus: So, I thought we could make our own book for the library: 'Great STEM women'.

Talk with a partner. Can you match the team member to the skill? The first one has been done for you. You may need to use a team member's name more than once!

1 **Zara's** skill was to explain what the team's ideas were before the project started.

2 ....'s skill was to suggest a practical action for the team to take.

3 ....'s skill was to identify facts that the team had learnt.

4 ....'s skill was to identify a contribution made by another team member.

5 ....'s skill was to summarise what had been learnt.

Starter activity

The topic I am working on today is:

....

Marcus, Sofia, Arun and Zara have made a group decision to create a book to improve other children's knowledge and understanding of pioneering work done by women in STEM. The school has agreed to print one copy of the book for each class in the upper school, and two for the library.

These are the different tasks that the team decide they will need to do. They are not in the right order.

Write the text of each paragraph	Find suitable images to illustrate the book	Group the facts. Make a paragraph plan for each page, e.g. 'summary', 'early life', 'main achievement(s)', 'conclusion & quotes'
Print out and bind the books. Distribute to classes/ library	Decide who we are going to include in the book	Look at some examples of good biography texts
Identify maximum ten key facts about each STEM pioneer	Edit the text of each paragraph	Collate images and text – using publishing software

The team decide who should do each task, how they should do it, what order the tasks should be done in and how long each will take. Your teacher will give you a download containing their plan; so far, three of the steps are included in the table. Look at the table – as a class you will discuss what the team will need to do next.

Class discussion

1 What makes a good biography?
2 What information about the STEM pioneers do you think the team should include in their book?
3 How do you think they could divide up the tasks fairly?
4 How do you think they could take advantage of the fact that they are working as a team?

Main activity

Work in a group. Plan how your group would carry out the 'Women in STEM' book project. Look at the list of tasks to be done, and decide:

- Who in your team will do each of the tasks?
- How will they do it?
- In what order and for how long will they do it?

Complete the table. Your team has one lesson plus private study time in which to finish the project, so try to make sure that everything can be done in that time.

Class discussion

1 What challenges did you face when working as a team to complete the plan, and how did you overcome them?
2 What teamwork skills did you use?
3 What teamwork skills can you still get better at?
4 If you were going to do this activity again, how could you do things differently?

Peer feedback

Show your completed team plan to someone from a different group, and ask them to tell you the answers to these questions:

1 Has the team included everything that needs to be done? YES/NO
2 Has the team chosen the best order to complete each of the tasks? YES/NO
3 According to the plan, is everyone in the team doing their fair share of the work? YES/NO
4 Can the project be completed in the time available? YES/NO

If the answer to any of the questions is 'NO', what changes could you make to the plan? (Write what they tell you here):

....

....

....

Independent reflection activity

Check your learning goals

If you are sure you have met them and can give a reason why put a '★'.

If you think you have met them put a '☺'.

If you think you are not quite there yet put a '😐'.

9

Getting better at reflection skills: Lesson 9

Reflection learning objectives

4.2 Teamwork

4.3 Personal viewpoints

Lesson learning goals

These are the goals for this lesson.
You will return to this table at the end of the lesson for the independent reflection activity.

My learning goals To get better at:	I think	My teacher/ partner thinks
explaining the benefits and challenges of working as a team to achieve a goal		
explaining how my ideas about a topic have changed as a result of what I've learnt		

Prior learning

Marcus is thinking of how he could finish the sentence 'All good teams . . . '

What words come to your mind when you think about teamwork? How many relevant ideas can you add to your mind-map? Your teacher will set you a time limit.

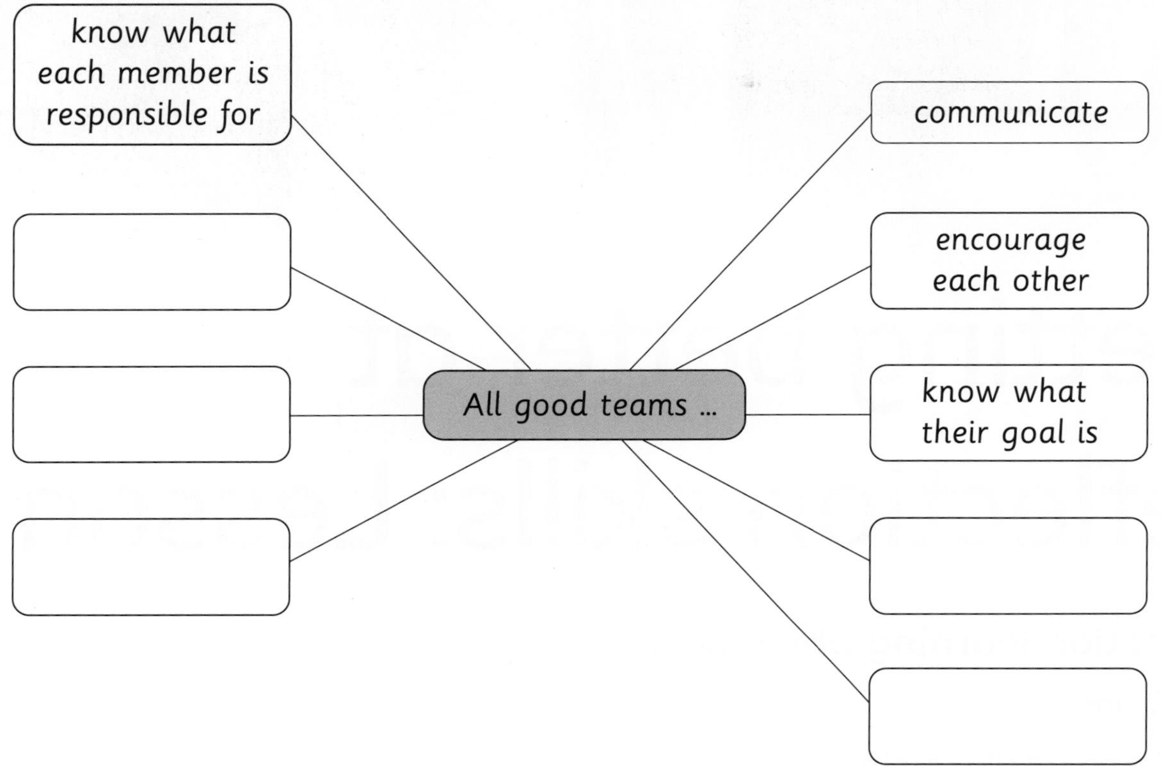

Talk with a partner. Explain why you chose these words to put in your mind-map.

Starter activity

The topic I am working on today is:

....

As part of a presentation to their year group, Sofia's group members are going to role play a press conference. They are going to play the roles of Valentina Tereshkova and the journalists to show the challenges they faced and explain how these were overcome.

In your group, rehearse a press conference like Sofia's. Every member of your group should take part. Choose a STEM pioneer, and decide who will act in role as her and who will act in role as the journalists.

Perform your press conference to the rest of the class.

Main activity

Think about the teamwork activities that you have experienced in this lesson, and in Lessons 7 and 8.

1 Think of one example of something that went well for you and your group.

Tell a partner:

- a What happened?
- b Why do you think it happened?
- c How could you make sure it happens again?

2 Think of one example of something that didn't go so well for you and your group.

Tell a partner:

a What happened?
b Why do you think it happened?
c How could you make it better in future?

Class discussion

1 How have your ideas about teamwork changed?
2 What experiences (positive and negative) have helped you to change your ideas about teamwork?

Independent reflection activity

Check your learning goals

If you are sure you have met them and can give a reason why put a '★'.

If you think you have met them put a '☺'.

If you think you are not quite there yet put a '😐'.

Self-assessment Lessons 7–9

How will I know if I have achieved my learning goals?

Use this activity to reflect on how well you have progressed over the last three lessons.

Tick (✓) 'Achieved' if you are sure you have made good progress with this skill and can give an example.

Tick (✓) 'Not there yet / with help' if you need some further practice so that you can make more progress.

If you tick 'Achieved', then challenge yourself to make further progress in the next section.

If you tick 'Not there yet / with help', there will be the chance to consolidate this skill in future lessons.

Continued

Reflection learning objectives To get better at:	Not there yet / with help	Achieved	Example
reflecting on personal contribution			
reflecting on teamwork			
reflecting on personal viewpoints			
reflecting on personal learning			

Reflect on your responses in your self-assessment and identify one area for improvement.

One area I want to improve in is:

....

How I will improve:

....

Challenge topic review

Think about the Challenge topic you have been exploring and complete the following statements.

I was surprised to discover/explore that ....

....

I did not know ....

....

I now think ....

....

1

Starting with collaboration skills: Lesson 1

Collaboration learning objectives

5.1 Cooperation and interdependence

5.2 Engaging in teamwork

Lesson learning goals

These are the goals for this lesson.
You will return to this table at the end of the lesson for the independent reflection activity.

My learning goals To start to:	I think	My teacher/ partner thinks
work well with other team members to achieve our team's goal		

Prior learning

Think about your answers to these questions about working in a group:

1 When your teacher asks you to work in a group, which do you prefer?

  a To choose the other people in the group yourself

  b To let the teacher decide who will be in the group

2 What are the advantages and disadvantages of (a)?

3 What are the advantages and disadvantages of (b)?

Talk with a partner. Tell your partner your answers to these questions. Does your partner agree or disagree?

Starter activity

As part of their class topic on healthy eating, Arun and his group have decided to do a research project on vegetables. As they discussed the topic, they realised there were some things that they don't know about vegetables. Read their discussion:

My mum always tells me to eat vegetables. She says they're good for me, but she never explains why!

I really like tomatoes, but are they vegetables? They look like fruit!

Besides tomatoes, my favourite vegetables are onions, but I don't think any of my friends like them!

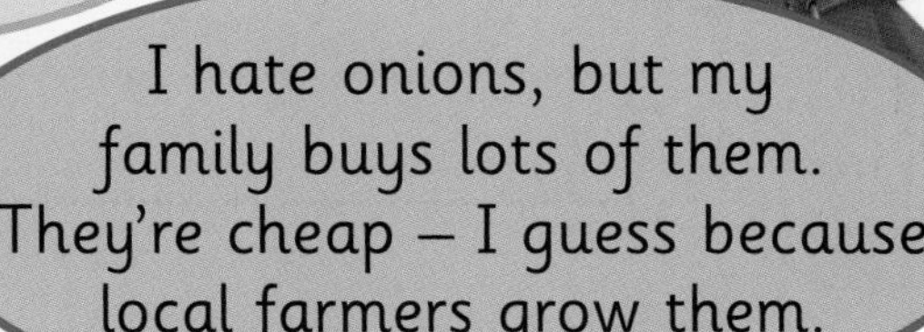

Following their discussion, the group's goal was to come up with four questions that they would like to find answers to by using their research skills:

Questions	Who suggested it?
a What is a vegetable (and what is not)?	
b What vegetables do our classmates like best?	
c Where do our vegetables come from?	
d Why is it healthy to eat vegetables?	

Read the discussion again. Based on what they say in the discussion, which group member do you think came up with each of these questions?

Class discussion

1 What answers would you give if you were asked these questions?

2 How could you check to find out if your answers are correct?

Main activity

The topic I am working on today is:

....

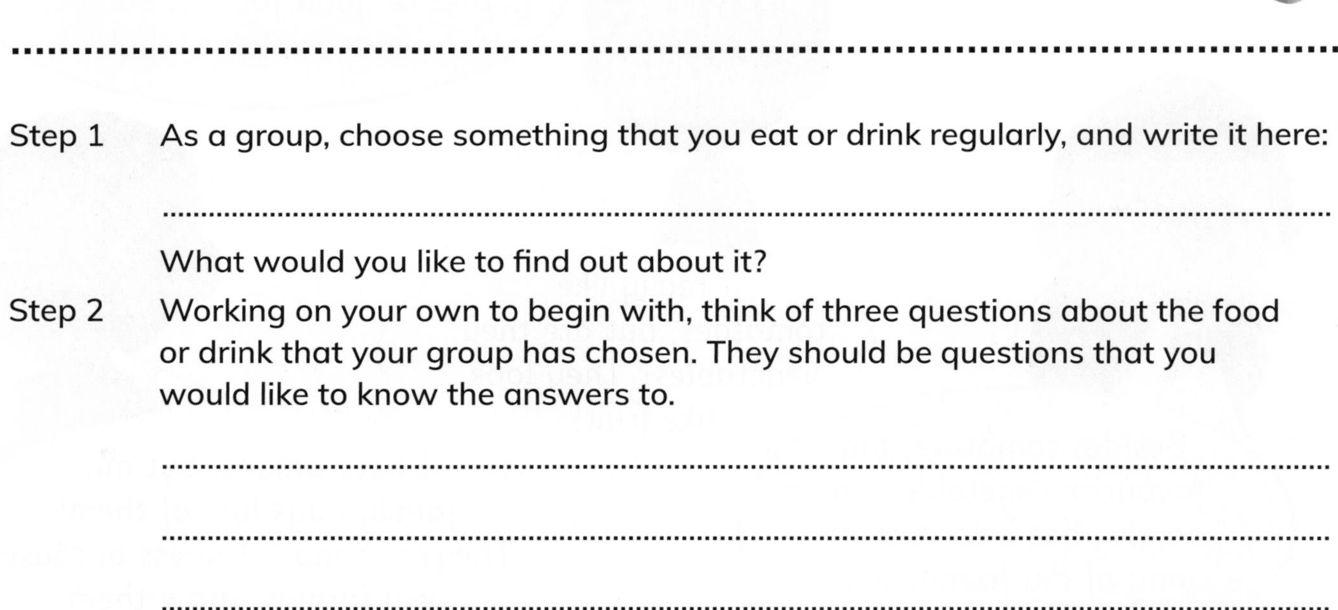

Step 1 As a group, choose something that you eat or drink regularly, and write it here:

....

What would you like to find out about it?

Step 2 Working on your own to begin with, think of three questions about the food or drink that your group has chosen. They should be questions that you would like to know the answers to.

....

....

....

Step 3 Now discuss your questions with the others in your group. Your group's goal is to write down four questions that your group will research about your chosen food or drink. Write them in the table below:

	Questions	Suggested by
1		
2		
3		
4		

How well did you and the others in your group collaborate to complete this activity?

Everyone agreed what food or drink to research. YES/NO

Everyone had the opportunity to suggest questions. YES/NO

Everyone agreed about what four questions to research. YES/NO

Class discussion

1 If the answer to any of the questions about collaboration was 'No', how did your group make decisions?

2 How can groups make decisions if some group members disagree?

Independent reflection activity

Check your learning goals

If you are sure you have met them and can give a reason why put a '★'.

If you think you have met them put a '☺'.

If you think you are not quite there yet put a '😐'.

Starting with collaboration skills: Lesson 2

Collaboration learning objectives

5.1 Cooperation and interdependence

5.2 Engaging in teamwork

Lesson learning goals

These are the goals for this lesson.
You will return to this table at the end of the lesson for the independent reflection activity.

My learning goals To start to:	I think	My teacher/ partner thinks
identify what tasks each team member will do in order to achieve our team's goal		
work well with other team members to achieve our team's goal		

Prior learning

In your opinion, what are the main advantages of working in a group?

Give each of the following a number from 1 (most important) to 5 (least important).

- Getting to know other people better ☐
- Sharing the work with other people, so you don't have to do so much on your own ☐
- Getting new ideas and learning new skills from other people ☐
- Being able to do things with other people that you couldn't do on your own ☐
- Learning to communicate better with other people ☐

Talk with a partner. Do you agree about what are the most important advantages? What other advantages of working in a group are there?

Starter activity

Look again at the questions Arun's group decided to research about vegetables in the Starter activity of Lesson 1.

Arun's group are now discussing where they can find answers to their questions. Read the discussion.

Marcus

Let's interview some adults about eating healthily – the people who cook our school meals, for example, or a doctor.

Arun

All of us could help to carry out a survey so that we ask each member of our class.

Sofia

I think we could find some useful information online if we search for 'vegetable' or 'fruit'.

Zara

Why don't we go to the supermarket and look at the labels on the packs of vegetables?

Which question in the Starter activity in Lesson 1 (a, b, c or d) is each group member talking about?

Arun ☐ Marcus ☐ Sofia ☐ Zara ☐

Class discussion

Arun thinks that it would be best if the whole group carries out a survey of their classmates to find out the answer to Question b in Lesson 1. Why does he think this?

Look at the other group members' suggestions.

1 When would it be better for two or more members of the group to work together to find the answer?

2 When could just one person do the work on their own?

Main activity

The topic I am working on today is:

....

Work in a group. Look again at the questions that your group agreed to research in the Main activity of Lesson 1.

How could you find the answers to these questions? Discuss with your group the ways that you could find answers to each question. Write down in the table one or more ways that your group will try to find answers.

Table 1

Our group's questions	How we will try to find the answer to our questions
a	
b	
c	
d	

Now, your goal is to decide who in your group will try to find the answer to each question.

Think about the class discussion you have just had. Would it sometimes be better if two or more group members work together to answer a question, or should everyone work on their own? Try to divide up the work fairly, so that everyone in the group has something to do, but no one has too much to do!

Discuss this with your group and write down your group's decisions here:

Table 2

Our group's questions	Who will try to find the answer to each question?
a	
b	
c	
d	

Peer feedback

Talk with a partner from another group. Show your partner your completed Table 2 and explain how your group has divided up the work.
Ask your partner to look at these statements and tick 'YES' or 'NO':

1 We have divided up the work fairly. YES/NO

2 Sometimes group members will work together. YES/NO

3 Sometimes group members will work on their own. YES/NO

Independent reflection activity

Check your learning goals

If you are sure you have met them and can give a reason why put a '★'.

If you think you have met them put a '☺'.

If you think you are not quite there yet put a '😐'.

Self-assessment Lessons 1–2

How will I know if I have achieved my learning goals?

Use this activity to reflect on how well you have progressed over the last two lessons.

Tick (✓) 'Achieved' if you are sure you have made good progress with this skill and can give an example.

Tick (✓) 'Not there yet / with help' if you need some further practice so that you can make more progress.

Continued

If you tick 'Achieved', then challenge yourself to make further progress in the next section.

If you tick 'Not there yet / with help', there will be the chance to consolidate this skill in future lessons.

Collaboration learning objectives To start to:	Not there yet / with help	Achieved	Example
develop cooperation and interdependence			
engage in teamwork			

Reflect on your responses in your self-assessment and identify one area for improvement.

One area I want to improve in is:

....

How I will improve:

....

Challenge topic review

Think about the Challenge topic you have been exploring and complete the following statements.

I was surprised to discover/explore that ....

....

I did not know ....

....

I now think ....

....

Developing collaboration skills: Lesson 3

Collaboration learning objectives

5.1 Cooperation and interdependence

5.2 Engaging in teamwork

Lesson learning goals

These are the goals for this lesson.
You will return to this table at the end of the lesson for the independent reflection activity.

My learning goals To develop my knowledge and understanding about:	I think	My teacher/ partner thinks
how to give each team member different tasks in order to achieve the team's goal		
how to work well in a team, for example by suggesting ideas that help us to achieve our goal		

Prior learning

Sofia asked Arun some questions about being a group leader. Unfortunately, Arun's answers have got mixed up. Match each answer to the correct question. One has been done for you.

Sofia's questions

a What are the advantages of having someone in the group who is the leader?

b What are the disadvantages?

c In order to be a good leader, what should the leader of the group do?

d What shouldn't they do?

Arun's answers	**Matches question (a–d)**
• Group members won't feel inspired to do their best by a group leader who makes decisions independently and just tells the others what to do.	4
• A leader who gives all the group members a chance to speak, and listens carefully to their ideas, can make everyone feel part of the group.	
• Having a group leader means that decisions can be made more quickly so that everyone in the group knows what they have to do.	
• If some group members don't agree with the leader, they might not feel like doing their best work, and the group might not achieve its goal.	

Talk with a partner. Do you agree with Arun's answers? What answers would you give to Sofia's questions?

Starter activity

The topic I am working on today is:

....

Arun and his group have done some research to answer the questions about vegetables that they asked in the Starter activity of Lesson 1. For each of their questions, they have collected different types of data. Now they are discussing how to present their findings to the class.

Read the suggestions that they make.

Now look back at the four questions in Lesson 1.
Which question is each group member talking about?

Class discussion

1 Which of the suggested ways of presenting their findings would need the most work to prepare? Why?
2 Which would need the least work? Why?
3 How could the work be divided fairly between the members of the group?

Main activity

Arun's group have made a plan of the presentation they will make to the class:

Our group's presentation about vegetables (Arun, Marcus, Sofia, Zara)

1 Introduction: Explain differences between vegetables and fruit (poster)

2 Explain benefits of eating vegetables (video)

3 Show the favourite vegetables in this class (pictogram)

4 Explain where our vegetables come from (world map)

5 Conclusion: Give out badges with the message 'Eat more vegetables for a healthy life!'

Work in a group. Your goal is to suggest a way that Arun's group can prepare and deliver their presentation so that the work is divided fairly between the group members. Complete the table to show how this can be done. Remember that sometimes it might be better for group members to work together on a task, and sometimes a team member might be able to do a task on their own.

Group member	Tasks to do to prepare for the presentation	Tasks to do during the presentation
Arun		
Marcus		
Sofia		
Zara		

Report back to the class, explaining how you have divided the tasks between the group members. Listen to what other groups say, and comment on how successful you think their solutions are.

Independent reflection activity

Check your learning goals

If you are sure you have met them and can give a reason why put a '★'.

If you think you have met them put a '☺'.

If you think you are not quite there yet put a '😐'.

Developing collaboration skills: Lesson 4

Collaboration learning objectives

5.1 Cooperation and interdependence

5.2 Engaging in teamwork

Lesson learning goals

These are the goals for this lesson.
You will return to this table at the end of the lesson for the independent reflection activity.

My learning goals To develop my knowledge and understanding about:	I think	My teacher/ partner thinks
how to give each team member different tasks in order to achieve our team's goal		
how to work well with other team members, and what ideas to suggest that will help our team to achieve its goal		

Prior learning

A group of students is planning to give a presentation to their class about a topic. The students in the group (A, B, C, D) have different skills.

Skills

Student A is good at drawing and designing things.

Student B is one of the best writers in the class.

Student C plays a musical instrument.

Student D is good at maths and science.

The group members decide what to include in each section of their presentation. Who would be the best student(s) to prepare each section? When might it be better for two or more students to work together? Write your answers (A, B, C or D, or more than one of these) next to each task below.

1 A report giving facts about the topic

2 A poster with text and pictures about the topic

3 A graph showing statistics about the topic

4 A song with words about the topic

Talk with a partner. Tell your partner your answers to these questions. Does your partner agree or disagree? Which of the tasks above would you like to do? Why?

Starter activity

The topic I am working on today is:

....

Imagine that your group is going to give a presentation about the food or drink you chose in the Main activity of Lesson 1. In your presentation, your goal is to give your audience more information about your chosen food or drink, and to encourage them to include it as part of their diet.

Look at the Choice Board on the download that your teacher will give you. As a group, choose six activities that you could do to prepare for your presentation. When you choose, think about:

- what would help to make your presentation more informative
- what might persuade your audience to include your food/drink in their diet
- what would make your presentation more interesting or exciting
- the different skills that members of your group have.

Cut out the six activities that your group has chosen, and stick them on the pyramid diagram that your teacher will give you. Order them from 'most useful' to 'useful'.

Class discussion

Report to the class, telling them which activities you have chosen.

Why did you choose each activity?

Main activity

Look at the plan that Arun's group made in the Main activity in Lesson 3. Working as a group, make a similar plan for your group's presentation about your chosen food or drink, including at least four of the things you chose from the Choice Board in the Starter activity in this lesson.

On your plan, show:

1 The order of the different sections of your presentation
2 Who will present and/or take part in each section

Peer feedback

Show your group's plan to a partner from a different group. Explain what your group decided to include in each of the different sections of your presentation and why. Explain also how you decided who would present each section.

Ask your partner to respond to each of these statements by choosing 'Yes' or 'No'.

1 Our group's presentation will:

- give the audience information about our chosen food or drink YES/NO
- persuade the audience to include our chosen food or drink in their diet YES/NO
- keep the audience's attention by being interesting and/or exciting. YES/NO

2 When giving the presentation, each member of the group will:

- do an equal share of the work YES/NO
- be able to do or show something they are good at. YES/NO

If any of the answers are 'NO', what improvements could you make to your presentation?

Independent reflection activity

Check your learning goals

If you are sure you have met them and can give a reason why put a '★'.

If you think you have met them put a '☺'.

If you think you are not quite there yet put a '😐'.

Self-assessment Lessons 3–4

How will I know if I have achieved my learning goals?

Use this activity to reflect on how well you have progressed over the last two lessons.

Tick (✓) 'Achieved' if you are sure you have made good progress with this skill and can give an example.

Tick (✓) 'Not there yet / with help' if you need some further practice so that you can make more progress.

If you tick 'Achieved', then challenge yourself to make further progress in the next section.

Continued

If you tick 'Not there yet / with help', there will be the chance to consolidate this skill in future lessons.

Collaboration learning objectives To develop my knowledge and understanding about:	Not there yet / with help	Achieved	Example
cooperation and interdependence			
engaging in teamwork			

Reflect on your responses in your self-assessment and identify one area for improvement.

One area I want to improve in is:

....

How I will improve:

....

Challenge topic review

Think about the Challenge topic you have been exploring and complete the following statements.

I was surprised to discover/explore that ....

....

I did not know ....

....

I now think ....

....

5

Getting better at collaboration skills: Lesson 5

Collaboration learning objectives

5.1 Cooperation and interdependence

5.2 Engaging in teamwork

Lesson learning goals

These are the goals for this lesson.
You will return to this table at the end of the lesson for the independent reflection activity.

My learning goals To get better at:	I think	My teacher/ partner thinks
giving each team member different tasks in order to achieve our team's goal		
working with other team members, and suggesting ideas that will help our team to achieve its goal		

Prior learning

Arun, Marcus, Zara and Sofia are planning to give a presentation to their year group about children's right to an education. They have different skills that they would like to develop and different prior experience.

Skills

Zara wants to improve her skills at writing **non-fiction** for an audience.

Arun wants to get better at designing visual material for a purpose.

Marcus wants to develop his musical performances in front of an audience.

Sofia wants to improve her data presentation skills.

Prior experience

Arun performed with the school choir at the last concert.

Sofia made a poster to advertise an athletics tournament.

Marcus has written a report about an experiment he did in Science Club.

Zara made a spreadsheet showing the amount (in grams) of plastic collected on a litter pick for a week.

Continued

The team decide what to include in each section of their presentation. Who would be the best team members to help each other prepare each section? Choose the best pair to work together on each task. The first one has been done for you.

1 A sticker with a slogan and a logo against child labour. Arun can work with Sofia.

2 A graph showing statistics about child poverty. .... can work with

....

3 A report giving facts about child poverty. .... can work with

....

4 Performing a song with words about child labour. .... can work with

....

Talk with a partner. Tell your partner your answers to these questions. Does your partner agree or disagree? Which of the tasks talked about would develop your skills further? Why?

Starter activity

You have planned presentations before in this unit. This activity is similar, but there are two extra challenges.

1 Last time your audience was children your age. This time they are younger.

2 Last time you relied on skills that your group members had already. This time you will need to plan for your group to develop new skills.

Imagine that your group is going to give a presentation about children's rights to children two years younger. In your presentation, your goal is to give your audience more information about how many children across the world have to work to support their families. You want them to understand that their right to an education is being denied.

The topic I am working on today is:

....

Look at the Choice Board below. As a group, choose four activities that you could do to prepare for your presentation. When you choose, think about:

- what would help to make your presentation more informative
- what might persuade your audience to take children's rights seriously
- what would make your presentation more interesting or exciting
- new skills that members of your group could develop by doing them.

Tick (✓) the activities you have chosen.

Skills Key:

Writing (factual)	Speaking clearly and expressively	Mathematical skills
Writing (imaginative)	Visual presentation	Geography skills
Research skills	Musical communication	Technology skills

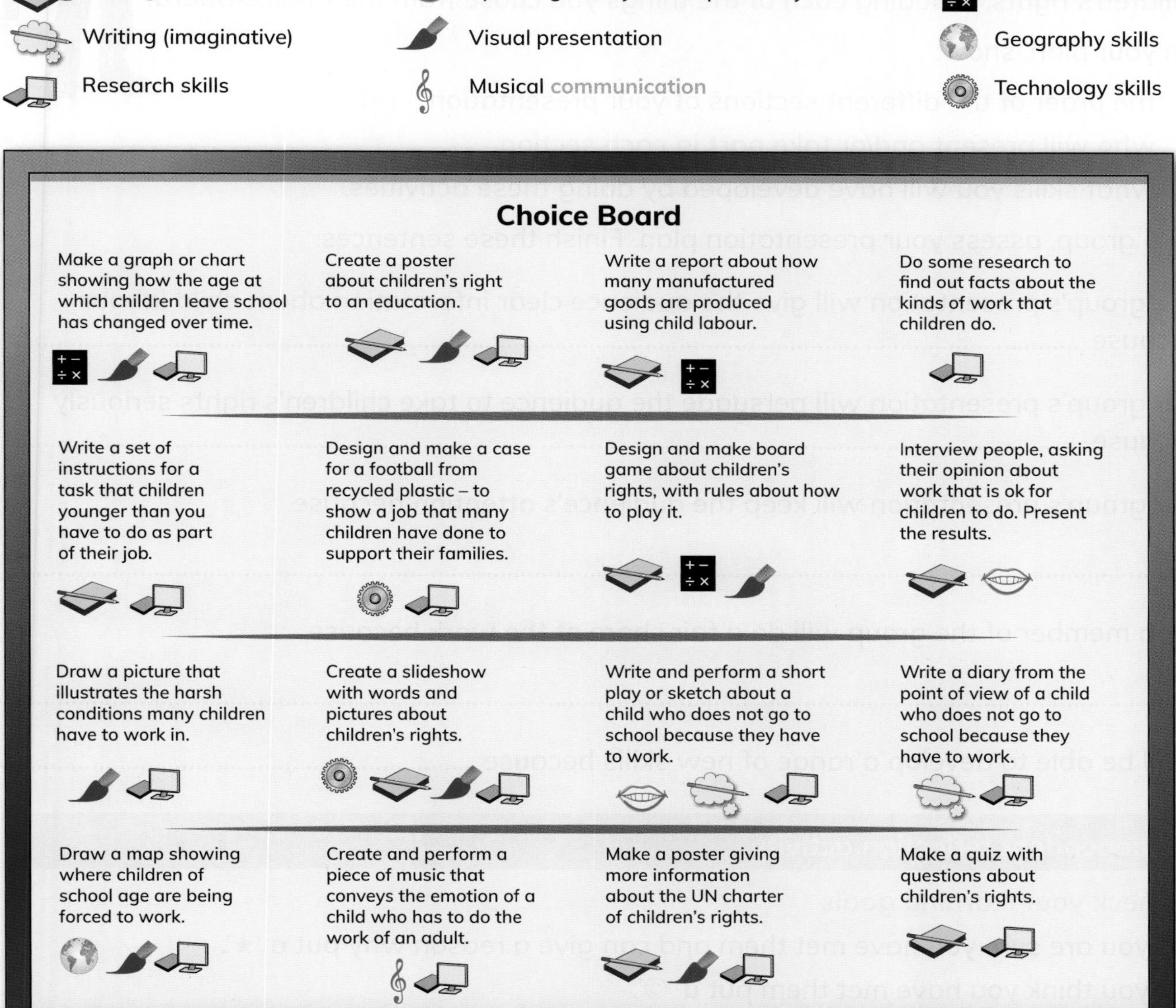

Choice Board

Make a graph or chart showing how the age at which children leave school has changed over time.	Create a poster about children's right to an education.	Write a report about how many manufactured goods are produced using child labour.	Do some research to find out facts about the kinds of work that children do.
Write a set of instructions for a task that children younger than you have to do as part of their job.	Design and make a case for a football from recycled plastic – to show a job that many children have done to support their families.	Design and make board game about children's rights, with rules about how to play it.	Interview people, asking their opinion about work that is ok for children to do. Present the results.
Draw a picture that illustrates the harsh conditions many children have to work in.	Create a slideshow with words and pictures about children's rights.	Write and perform a short play or sketch about a child who does not go to school because they have to work.	Write a diary from the point of view of a child who does not go to school because they have to work.
Draw a map showing where children of school age are being forced to work.	Create and perform a piece of music that conveys the emotion of a child who has to do the work of an adult.	Make a poster giving more information about the UN charter of children's rights.	Make a quiz with questions about children's rights.

Class discussion

Report to the class, telling them which activities you have chosen.

1 Why did you choose each activity?
2 What skills will you develop by doing them?

Main activity

Look at the plan that your group made in the Main activity in Lesson 4. Working as a group, make a similar plan for your group's presentation about children's rights, including each of the things you chose from the Choice Board.

On your plan, show:

- the order of the different sections of your presentation
- who will present and/or take part in each section
- what skills you will have developed by doing these activities.

As a group, assess your presentation plan. Finish these sentences:

Our group's presentation will give the audience clear information about child labour because ....

Our group's presentation will persuade the audience to take children's rights seriously because ....

Our group's presentation will keep the audience's attention because

....

Each member of the group will do a fair share of the work because

....

I will be able to develop a range of new skills because ....

Independent reflection activity

Check your learning goals

If you are sure you have met them and can give a reason why put a '★'.

If you think you have met them put a '☺'.

If you think you are not quite there yet put a '😐'.

Self-assessment Lesson 5

How will I know if I have achieved my learning goals?

Use this activity to reflect on how well you have progressed over the last lesson.

Tick (✓) 'Achieved' if you are sure you have made good progress with this skill and can give an example.

Tick (✓) 'Not there yet / with help' if you need some further practice so that you can make more progress.

If you tick 'Achieved', then challenge yourself to make further progress in the next section.

If you tick 'Not there yet / with help', there will be the chance to consolidate this skill in future lessons.

Collaboration learning objectives To get better at:	Not there yet / with help	Achieved	Example
cooperation and interdependence			
engaging in teamwork			

Reflect on your responses in your self-assessment and identify one area for improvement.

One area I want to improve in is:

....

How I will improve:

....

Challenge topic review

Think about the Challenge topic you have been exploring and complete the following statements.

I was surprised to discover/explore that ....

....

I did not know ....

....

I now think ....

....

1

Starting with communication skills: Lesson 1

Communication learning objectives

6.1 Communicating information

6.2 Listening and responding

Lesson learning goals

These are the goals for this lesson.
You will return to this table at the end of the lesson for the independent reflection activity.

My learning goals To start to:	I think	My teacher/ partner thinks
be clear and relevant when talking about a topic		
respond to what someone says in a class discussion by asking them a question		

Prior learning

Zara's group were having a discussion about an idea that Marcus came up with.

Zara: I think it is a positive idea. All ages will benefit.

Arun: I'm less convinced. I'm not everyone is ready for such a big change.

Marcus: If now is not the right time, when will be?

Sofia: Are you sure you have thought it through properly?

Who was positive about the idea? Who was less sure? Complete the table. The first one has been done for you.

Key

 Positive about the idea  Less sure about the idea

Team member	What they thought about the idea
Zara	
Arun	
Marcus	
Sofia	

Talk with a partner. What clues did you find that helped you decide how they felt?

When have you felt positive about an idea?

How did you tell someone else that you agreed with their idea?

When have you felt less positive about an idea?

How did you tell someone else that you did not agree with their idea?

Starter activity

The topic I am working on today is:

....

The topic Zara's group were discussing was ways to improve their school nature area. Read their discussion with a partner, and note down your answers to the questions ready for class discussion.

Class discussion

1 Who thought of a possible problem with one idea?
2 What was the idea, and what was the problem?
3 Can you think of any other possible problems?
4 Who thought of a reason to support someone else's idea?
5 What was the idea, and what was good about it?
6 Can you think of any other good points to any of the other ideas?

Main activity

Sofia and her group are looking at a plan they have made for a wildlife area that is going to be built in their school. Your teacher will give you this as a download. The bad news is that their work has got jumbled up. Now they can't remember what each of the zones will be used for!

Work in a group. Your teacher will give each group member some information that will help you to complete their plan. Tell the other group members your information, and listen carefully to what the others tell you. Add labels to the plan to show what each of the zones is.

Arun and Zara have been thinking about good listening.

Independent reflection activity

Check your learning goals

If you are sure you have met them and can give a reason why put a '★'.

If you think you have met them put a '☺'.

If you think you are not quite there yet put a '😐'.

Starting with communication skills: Lesson 2

Communication learning objectives

6.1 Communicating information

6.2 Listening and responding

Lesson learning goals

These are the goals for this lesson.
You will return to this table at the end of the lesson for the independent reflection activity.

My learning goals To start to:	I think	My teacher/ partner thinks
be clear and relevant when talking about a topic		
respond to what someone says in a class discussion by asking them a question		

Prior learning

Zara's group were still in discussion – this time about a different idea that Sofia came up with.

Zara — I am afraid I have come to the conclusion that it would, in fact, be a step backwards.

Marcus — I know not everyone is persuaded. But I am sure that the plus points outnumber the negatives.

Arun — Can we be sure it will work?

Sofia — If we don't give it a try, we'll never know.

Who was positive about the idea? Who was less sure? Complete the table. The first one has been done for you.

Key

 Positive about the idea

 Less sure about the idea

 Negative about the idea

Team member	What they thought about the idea
Zara	☹
Arun	
Marcus	
Sofia	

Talk with a partner. Work with a different partner from the person you worked with in the Prior learning activity for Lesson 1.

When have you felt positive about an idea?

How did you tell someone else that you agreed with their idea?

When have you felt less positive about an idea?

How did you tell someone else that you did not agree with their idea?

Starter activity

Your challenge is to think of reasons to support something.

1 Roll a die. Based on the number you roll, your teacher will give you an action to support.

2 Make your notes here:

The idea I am supporting is ....

My reasons for supporting this are ....

....

3 Swap ideas with as many others as possible who rolled the same number as you. Note their ideas here:

Reason 1 ....

Reason 2 ....

Reason 3 ....

Reason 4 ....

Reason 5 ....

Reason 6 ....

4 Complete these sentences:

The idea I am asking you to support is ....

There are several good reasons for this.

Firstly, you will all agree that ....

Secondly, ...

This is because ....

In addition, ...

Furthermore, ...

Finally, it is clear that ....

Main activity

The topic I am working on today is:

....

Step 1 As a group, think of something that could make the area around your school a better place for plants and animals to live.

Step 2 Work on your own to begin with. Think of ideas to support the group's suggestion. Make some notes.

Step 3 Discuss your ideas in your group. Your group's goal is to persuade others to support your idea. Listen to everyone else's suggestions and ask questions if there is anything you want to know or if something is not clear to you.

Step 4 On your own complete these sentences:

Our suggestion for how to make the area around our school a better place for plants and animals to live is ....

The first reason this would be a good idea is that ....

Secondly, it would help to ....

Finally, it would ....

Peer feedback

Talk to a partner in a different group about your ideas for how to make the area around our school a better place for plants and animals. Listen to their ideas and ask them questions to find out more:

Ask them to tell you two ideas that you explained clearly (write what they tell you here):

★ ....

★ ....

And one thing that could have been clearer (write what they tell you here):

....

Class discussion

What do you now think about what good listeners usually do?

Independent reflection activity

Check your learning goals

If you are sure you have met them and can give a reason why put a '★'.

If you think you have met them put a '☺'.

If you think you are not quite there yet put a '😐'.

Self-assessment Lessons 1–2

How will I know if I have achieved my learning goals?

Use this activity to reflect on how well you have progressed over the last two lessons.

Tick (✓) 'Achieved' if you are sure you have made good progress with this skill and can give an example.

Tick (✓) 'Not there yet / with help' if you need some further practice so that you can make more progress.

If you tick 'Achieved', then challenge yourself to make further progress in the next section.

If you tick 'Not there yet / with help', there will be the chance to consolidate this skill in future lessons.

Communication learning objectives To start to:	Not there yet / with help	Achieved	Example
communicate information			
listen and respond			

Continued

Reflect on your responses in your self-assessment and identify one area for improvement.

One area I want to improve in is:

....

How I will improve:

....

Challenge topic review

Think about the Challenge topic you have been exploring and complete the following statements.

I was surprised to discover/explore that ....

....

I did not know ....

....

I now think ....

....

Developing communication skills: Lesson 3

Communication learning objectives

6.1 Communicating information

6.2 Listening and responding

Lesson learning goals

These are the goals for this lesson.
You will return to this table at the end of the lesson for the independent reflection activity.

My learning goals To develop my knowledge and understanding about:	I think	My teacher/ partner thinks
how to present information about a topic in an organised way		
how to respond to what others say in class discussions by asking questions and/or sharing my own ideas		

Prior learning

Sofia and her group were asked to talk about why it is important to learn about nature.

Sofia: It is interesting to find out about how all of the plants grow. If we didn't know, we wouldn't know how to grow food!

Marcus: It's not *just* useful, though. There's a different feeling you have when you're in a wild place.

Zara: I know what you mean. It's special. What do you think, Arun?

Arun: We also need to learn about nature so we know how to protect it.

What would you say if you were part of the group?
Why is it important to learn about nature?

Discuss your ideas with a partner.

Starter activity

The topic I am working on today is:

....

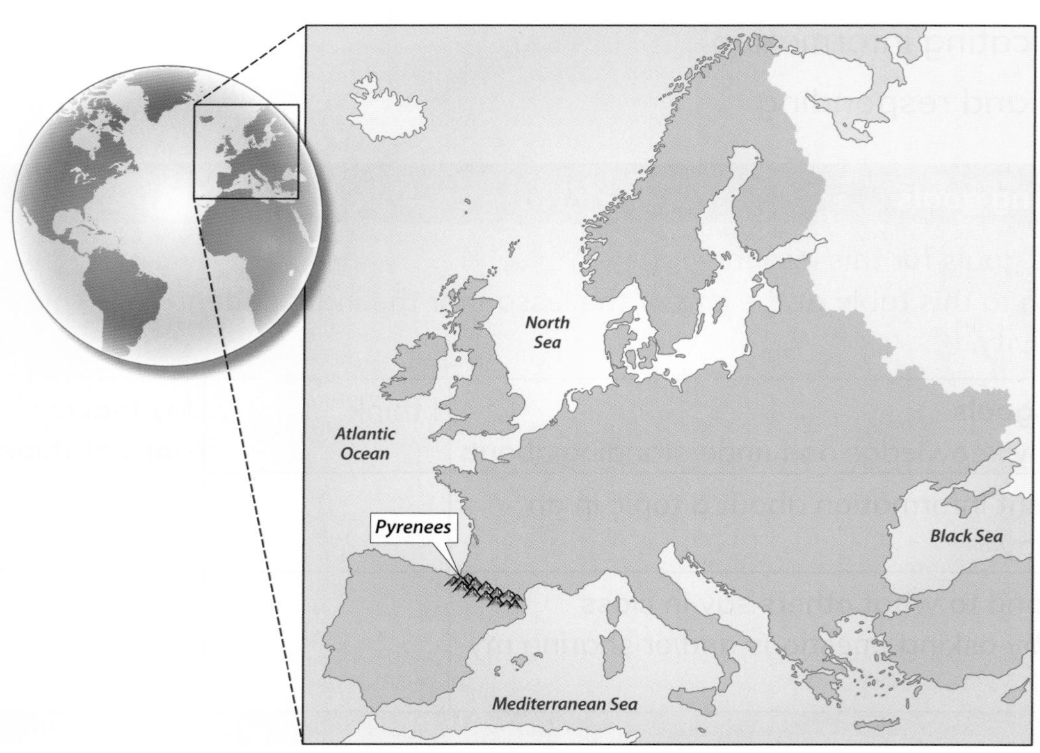

Background information: Bears had died out in the Pyrenees. They were brought back in to the region – but not everyone thought it was a good idea.

Read these two opinions.

Most farmers in our village are concerned about the bears.

Firstly, we are sheep farmers. As everyone knows bears scare sheep.

Secondly, our sheep graze on mountain slopes. When they run away from the bears they fall. Some of them die.

Thirdly, it is hard to make a living here. I want my children to have a future.

In conclusion, it is my belief that bears and sheep just do not mix.

Erik Etxebarria

All **conservationists** I know want the bears to stay.

Firstly, they have a right to be here. They only died out because of people.

Secondly, they wear tracking devices so we know where they are.

Thirdly, in summer the bears mainly live off fruit so they don't bother sheep.

In conclusion, it is my belief that bears, sheep and farmers can get along just fine.

Monica Goikoetxea

If you could meet Erik and Monica, what would you ask them so that you could find out more? Work with a partner.

Here are two to start you off:

- Monica, can you please tell us more about how the tracking devices help?
- Erik, could you explain what the problem is for your children please?

Main activity

You will now ask your questions to 'Erik' and 'Monica' in turn. Listen to what they say and make notes on a sheet of paper. Then complete the statements below.

Erik Etxebarria is concerned about the bears staying because	Monica Goikoetxea is concerned about the bears going away because ....
He also is worried that	She also is worried that ....
He wants	She wants ....
This is because	This is because ....

Class discussion

How would you complete Arun and Zara's sentences now?

Independent reflection activity

Check your learning goals

If you are sure you have met them and can give a reason why put a '★'.

If you think you have met them put a '☺'.

If you think you are not quite there yet put a '😐'.

Developing communication skills: Lesson 4

Communication learning objectives

6.1 Communicating information

6.2 Listening and responding

Lesson learning goals

These are the goals for this lesson.
You will return to this table at the end of the lesson for the independent reflection activity.

My learning goals To develop my knowledge and understanding about:	I think	My teacher/ partner thinks
how to present information about a topic in an organised way		
how to respond to what others say in class discussions by asking questions and/or sharing my own ideas		

Prior learning

Marcus and his group were thinking of rules for how to behave when looking at plants and animals near the school.

Marcus: I think we will need to be quiet otherwise they will get frightened.

Sofia: You're right. In any case, if we're too noisy, we won't see any at all.

Zara: We'll need to wash our hands afterwards.

Arun: I know! If we find nests, we must mark them on our map but we must leave them alone.'

What would you say if you were part of the group?

Discuss your ideas with a partner.

Starter activity

The topic I am working on today is:

....

Arun is taking part in a debate because his class are being given a choice of activity. He thinks that the class should choose the nature walk. He has prepared a presentation with a clear structure.

Using Arun's numbers (1–4), give each part of his presentation a number to show its structure. You may need to use a number more than once! An example has been done for you.

My presentation structure

1 Introduction
2 Arguments for (reasons to support my idea)
3 Arguments against (reasons not to support my idea)
4 Conclusion

a	Good morning. I think that a nature walk would be a good choice. Let me explain.	1
b	It will be interesting to find out what plants and creatures are out there. It will be fun, and it will be exercise too!	
c	We do know about a lot of plants and animals from books. How much do we know about what lives locally?	
d	Some people might say that there isn't enough time.	
e	However, learning about biology is an important part of science!	
f	So to give yourself the chance to find out about plants and animals *for yourself*, I urge you all to vote for the nature walk.	

Main activity

Arun's group helped him develop his presentation.
They used a skeleton plan to organise their ideas.

Now it is your turn. Look back to the Main activity in Lesson 2 where you thought of something that could make the area around your school a better place for plants and animals to live. Remind yourself of the ideas that you came up with. Now use the blank skeleton plan that your teacher will give you to develop your ideas. You can see their plan on the next page.

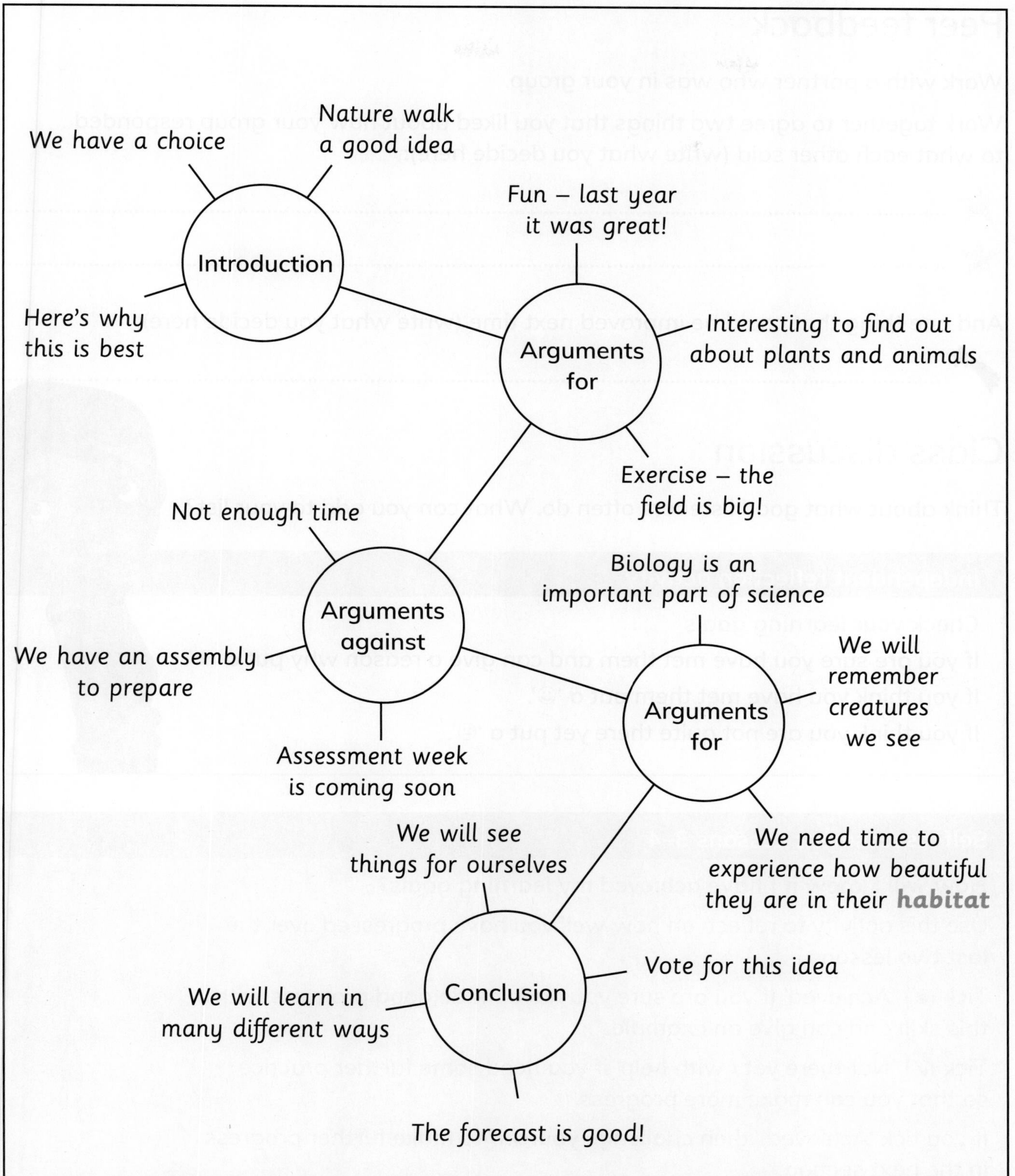
Introduction
We have a choice
Nature walk a good idea
Here's why this is best
Arguments for
Fun – last year it was great!
Interesting to find out about plants and animals
Exercise – the field is big!
Arguments against
Not enough time
We have an assembly to prepare
Assessment week is coming soon
Arguments for
Biology is an important part of science
We will remember creatures we see
We need time to experience how beautiful they are in their **habitat**
Conclusion
We will see things for ourselves
Vote for this idea
We will learn in many different ways
The forecast is good!

Peer feedback

Work with a partner who was in your group.

Work together to agree two things that you liked about how your group responded to what each other said (write what you decide here):

★ ....

★ ....

And one thing that could be improved next time (write what you decide here):

 ....

Class discussion

Think about what good listeners often do. What can you add to your list?

Independent reflection activity

Check your learning goals

If you are sure you have met them and can give a reason why put a '★'.

If you think you have met them put a '☺'.

If you think you are not quite there yet put a '😐'.

Self-assessment Lessons 3–4

How will I know if I have achieved my learning goals?

Use this activity to reflect on how well you have progressed over the last two lessons.

Tick (✓) 'Achieved' if you are sure you have made good progress with this skill and can give an example.

Tick (✓) 'Not there yet / with help' if you need some further practice so that you can make more progress.

If you tick 'Achieved', then challenge yourself to make further progress in the next section.

Continued

If you tick 'Not there yet / with help', there will be the chance to consolidate this skill in future lessons.

Communication learning objectives To develop my knowledge and understanding about:	Not there yet / with help	Achieved	Example
communicating information			
listening and responding			

Reflect on your responses in your self-assessment and identify one area for improvement.

One area I want to improve in is:

....

How I will improve:

....

Challenge topic review

Think about the Challenge topic you have been exploring and complete the following statements.

I was surprised to discover/explore that ....

....

I did not know ....

....

I now think ....

....

5

Getting better at communication skills: Lesson 5

Communication learning objectives

6.1 Communicating information

6.2 Listening and responding

Lesson learning goals

These are the goals for this lesson.
You will return to this table at the end of the lesson for the independent reflection activity.

My learning goals To get better at:	I think	My teacher/ partner thinks
presenting information about a topic in a clear and organised way		
joining in discussions by asking relevant questions and sharing my own ideas		

Prior learning

Arun makes a list of the ways that he can show that he is listening carefully when someone else is speaking to him. Which of these do you think is the most important? Which do you think is the least important? Number each item on Arun's list from 1 (most important) to 6 (least important).

- Asking questions or making comments ☐
- Keeping still while the speaker is talking ☐
- Saying things like 'I see', 'I understand', etc. ☐
- Smiling or nodding to show you're paying attention ☐
- Making eye contact with the speaker ☐
- Allowing the speaker to finish what they're saying ☐

Talk with a partner. Did you both choose the same thing as 'most important'? Explain your choice to your partner. What else could you do to show that you're listening?

Starter activity

The topic I am working on today is:

....

The students in Zara's class have decided to make a donation to a charity that protects wildlife and nature. They do some research in order to decide which charity to give money to.

Read the information about a charity in the download that your teacher will give you, and think about your answers to the questions for the class discussion.

Class discussion

In your opinion:

1 What information is most important when deciding which charity to give money to?

2 What are the advantages of giving money to a local charity?

3 Is it better to make a large donation to one charity, or smaller donations to several different charities?

Main activity

Work in a group. Your group's goal is to decide which charity you would like to make a donation to using the information about different charities that each group member has been given.

Communicate the information you have been given about a charity to the others in your group. Listen to the information that other group members tell you about their charities. Remember to ask questions if there is anything that isn't clear to you or if you would like more information about something.

As a group, discuss which of the charities to make a donation to and reach a decision. Write the name of your chosen charity here:

....

Report your group's decision to the class, giving reasons why you chose this charity.

Independent reflection activity

Check your learning goals

If you are sure you have met them and can give a reason why put a '★'.

If you think you have met them put a '☺'.

If you think you are not quite there yet put a '😐'.

Self-assessment Lesson 5

How will I know if I have achieved my learning goals?

Use this activity to reflect on how well you have progressed over the last lesson.

Tick (✓) 'Achieved' if you are sure you have made good progress with this skill and can give an example.

Tick (✓) 'Not there yet / with help' if you need some further practice so that you can make more progress.

If you tick 'Achieved', then challenge yourself to make further progress in the next section.

If you tick 'Not there yet / with help', there will be the chance to consolidate this skill in future lessons.

Communication learning objectives To get better at:	Not there yet / with help	Achieved	Example
communicating information			
listening and responding			

Reflect on your responses in your self-assessment and identify one area for improvement.

One area I want to improve in is:

....

How I will improve:

....

Challenge topic review

Think about the Challenge topic you have been exploring and complete the following statements.

I was surprised to discover/explore that ....

....

I did not know ....

....

I now think ....

....

Glossary

acrostic	a text in which the first letters of each line spell out a word or phrase, which is usually the subject or topic of the text.
aggrieved	feeling unhappy, perhaps because of being treated unfairly
analysis	In general, looking at something in more detail, for example, in order to understand the different parts that it consists of. In Primary Global Perspectives, analysis may involve understanding different perspectives on a topic or issue, or how different causes and consequences are related to one another. Analysis may also involve understanding data presented as numbers or in the form of graphs, charts or tables.
beneficial	helpful or useful.
bias	having a strong personal opinion for or against something that affects your judgement of it.
biology	the study of living things.
blended learning	a way of learning that combines traditional classroom lessons with lessons that use computer technology and may be given over the internet.
blurb	a description of what a book is about, often found on the back cover of the book.
bug hotel	a structure created for the purpose of providing shelter for insects.
chemist	a person who studies chemistry, or a scientist who works with chemicals or studies their reactions.
child labour	the use of children to do work that should be done by adults.
closed questions	closed questions do not need a developed answer. Closed questions usually have a limited range of possible answers.

collaboration	Working together with other people to achieve a shared outcome or to resolve an issue or problem.
communication	Sending and responding to information by speaking, writing or using other media such as digital technologies. Communication also requires skills such as listening and reading so that information can be received.
compost	a mixture of decayed leaves and plants that is added to the soil to improve its quality.
conservationists	someone who believes that people should protect nature
consolidate	to pull together and strengthen, e.g. your knowledge and understanding.
cosmonaut	a person who travelled into space from the Soviet Union (and, later, Russia); a person who travels into space from the United States, Canada, Europe, and Japan is called an astronaut and a person who travels into space from China is called a taikonaut.
data	information, especially numbers or facts
decaying	to gradually become bad or weak or be destroyed, often because of natural causes like bacteria or age.
e-reader	a small electronic device with a screen that allows you to read books in an electronic form.
elated	feeling very happy
evaluate / evaluation	to study something carefully and decide how good or bad it is.
excerpt	a short part taken from a longer text.
Gross Domestic Product	the total value of goods and services that a country produces in a year.
habitat	the natural environment of an animal or plant.
in role	when you are 'in role', you are like the person an actor represents in a film or a play. You are pretending to be that person.

logo	a design or symbol used by a company to advertise its product or a campaign group to convey a message.
malaria	a disease that you can get from the bite of a particular type of mosquito.
meadow	a field of grass, often with flowers.
mind-map	a type of diagram (= simple plan) with lines and circles for organising information so that it is easier to use or remember.
non-fiction	writing that is about real events and facts, rather than stories that have been invented.
open questions	Open questions sometimes need a developed answer. Open questions also sometimes have a wide range of possible answers.
per capita	for each person.
perspective	a point of view on an issue. People can have different perspectives for many reasons, including what they believe to be true or right.
potential	a potential problem, employer, partner, etc. may become one in the future, although they are not one now: a potential employer may become an employer in the future.
press conference	a meeting at which a person or organisation makes a public statement, and reporters can ask questions.
psychologists	someone who has studied the human mind and feelings.
Pyrenees	a mountain range that lies between France and Spain.
reflect/reflection	In general, to think about or consider something in depth. In Primary Global Perspectives, reflection may involve thinking about how well you have achieved your learning goals, how your thinking about an issue or your behaviour has changed, how much progress you have made in developing your skills, etc. You may also be expected to reflect on your personal contribution to a team effort, and on the benefits and challenges of working as a team.
reptile	a cold blooded animal whose body is covered with scales (like pieces of hard skin), for example a snake.

research In general, investigating an issue or topic in order to get information about it. In Primary Global Perspectives, research may involve making questions or predictions to help you find out more about an issue, finding sources that contain useful information, carrying out investigations using interviews and/or questionnaires, and presenting the results of an investigation.

role play pretending to be someone else, especially as part of learning a new skill.

slogan a short, easily remembered phrase, especially one used to advertise an idea or a product.

Soviet before 1992, Russia was part of a larger country called the Soviet Union. Things to do with this larger country were called 'Soviet'.

species a group of plants or animals that share similar characteristics.

STEM an abbreviation for Science, Technology, Engineering, Maths.

tuberculosis a serious infectious disease that can attack a person's body, especially their lungs.

typhus an infectious disease causing a high body temperature.

Venn diagram a diagram with overlapping circles for sorting items into two (or more) groups, while also allowing items to belong to more than one group by being placed in the overlapping section(s).